Our Motto:

*Once a week,
a meat loaf in
every oven*

FIFTY-TWO
MEAT LOAVES

Michael McLaughlin

A JOHN BOSWELL ASSOCIATES/KING HILL PRODUCTIONS BOOK

SIMON & SCHUSTER
NEW YORK   LONDON   TORONTO   SYDNEY   TOKYO   SINGAPORE

"Sally Schneider's Amazing Buttermilk Mashed Potatoes" appearing on page 123 is from *The Art of Low-Calorie Cooking,* copyright © 1990 by Sally Schneider. Reprinted by permission of Stewart, Tabori & Chang, Publishers.

A John Boswell Associates/King Hill Productions Book

SIMON & SCHUSTER
Simon & Schuster Building
Rockefeller Center
1230 Avenue of the Americas
New York, NY 10020

Designed by Barbara Cohen Aronica and Jan Halper Scaglia.
Typeset in Jackson, Michigan by Jackson Typesetting
Printed in Stevens Point, Wisconsin by Worzalla

10 9 8 7 6 5 4 3 2 1

Library of Congress Cataloging in Publication Data available on request
ISBN: 0-671-78539-7

*For all the moms,
including mine,
who make the meat loaves*

Acknowledgments

With grateful thanks to John Boswell, Susan Wyler, Patty Brown, Susan Lescher and Lisa Ekus, without whom I couldn't and wouldn't.

Contents

Introduction 10

Technique, Such As It Is 11

■ ■ ■

Chapter One 14

Coast to Coast:
Recipes for Good Old American Meat Loaves
From the hills of New England to the beaches of Hawaii, our favorites include Classic Interstate Meat Loaf, Firecracker BBQ Chicken Loaf, Pineapple Luau Loaf, Little Italy Pepperoni-Mushroom Pizza Loaf and many more.

■ ■ ■

Chapter Two 38

A View from Abroad:
Recipes with International Flavor
Meat Loaf is also a foreign affair, featuring such exotically seasoned specialities as Pretty Much Pâté, Sherried Teriyaki Turkey Loaf, Swedish Meat Loaf with Creamy Dilled Pan Gravy and Cold Veal Loaf with Tuna Mayonnaise.

■ ■ ■

Chapter Three 56

Upwardly Mobile Meat Loaves:
Recipes for the Modern Gourmet
Definitely not your mother's meat loaf, these products of the modern pantry include Two-Meat Loaf with Sun-Dried Tomatoes, Herb Garden Buttermilk Meat Loaf, Smoked Three-Meat Loaf, Venison Ring with Brandied Cherry Sauce and plenty of others.

■ ■ ■

Chapter Four 76

Meat Loaves of the Rich and Famous:
Recipes from the Celebrated
They're just like you and me—they love meat loaf, too, including such succulent fare as Ann Landers's Good Advice Meat Loaf, Ed Debevic's Burnt Diner Meat Loaf, Paul Prudhomme's Cajun Meat Loaf and Serendipity 3's Country Meat Loaf.

■ ■ ■

Chapter Five 96

Playing with Your Food:
Recipes That Entertain

More than mere meat loaves, these are as fun to create as they are tasty to eat. Among the ever-so-slightly ambitious loaves in this chapter are Veal Cordon Bleu Roulade, Egg-in-the-Middle Meat Loaf, Cranberry-Glazed Turkey Loaf with a Tunnel of Stuffing and Beef and Blue Cheese Mini-Muffin Loaves with Bacon.

■ ■ ■

Chapter Six 112

Alternative Loaf Styles:
Recipes for the Times in Which We Live

These loaves go beyond red meat, in such light, modern fare as Salmon Loaf with Basil Sauce, Shrimp and Chicken Loaf with Pink Tomato Cream, Lean Turkey Loaf with Caramelized Vegetables and Hearty Chicken Loaf with Whole Wheat Crumbs.

■ ■ ■

Chapter Seven 124

Fast Food:
Recipes from the Back of the Box

Some of the world's best—and easiest—meat loaves come from convenience recipes printed on the backs of product packages. These include Lipton's Souperior Meat Loaf, Emergency Pantry Meat Loaf, Vegetable Confetti Meat Loaf and Quick and Easy Ranch Loaf.

■ ■ ■

Index 140

Introduction

When the going gets tough, we all get hungry. Less than tranquil times sooner or later have everyone feeling the need for a little tender, loving care, and there is no more tender and lovable food than meat loaf. In a back-to-the-basics era, during what the networks might call "reality-based" programming, a savory, juicy and comforting meat loaf takes us back to safer, sweeter and saner times—and it just happens to taste good, too.

Of course, meat loaf can hardly be said to have returned, since it's never actually been gone. Coffee shops, diners and other equally functional eateries—immune to the passing whims of culinary fashion—have always given meat loaf a place of importance on their encyclopedic menus. In certain homes, it is true, meat loaf fell from favor—cholesterol jitters, pizza deliveries, single-serving microwaveable pouches and other ugly modern realities having rendered its preparation obsolete. In other homes, however (those with traditional values and/or resident carnivores), there was always meat loaf. It was frequently good and then sometimes not so good, but it was always edible and always comforting. This is not a compliment that can be paid to a $24 portion of seared foie gras with papaya when the chef is having an off day.

Still there is a meat loaf resurgence going on. Parallel with what is called The Diner Movement, I have perceived an increased interest in meat loaves at the "serious" food level. This revival is not limited to restaurants and the food pages of magazines: real people are also really interested once again in making great meat loaves at home. Cooking in and eating in are ideas whose time has come around again and so a collection of great meat loaf recipes seemed in order.

Fifty-Two Meat Loaves, then, is for cooks with kids who seek a meal the whole family can enjoy. It is for those cooks who love themes and variations on cherished family favorites. It is for those cooks who never think of fixing something at home until they've paid too much for it in a restaurant. It is for those who—temporarily, at least—find it economically advisable to monitor their cash flow but want to dine well nonetheless. And it is for those cooks—and eaters—who simply never get enough meat loaf. For them, and for you, here are fifty-two blues-banishing, nerve-calming, stomach-smiling meat loaves. Let's get cooking.

Technique, Such As It Is

Fare as carefree as meat loaf is pretty much without technique, but here are a few tips to help you turn out sublime meat loaf every time.

First, a meat loaf should be moist. If your cholesterol is in the safe zone, this moisture, along with flavor, can be supplied by the animal fat in ordinary supermarket ground meats. Ground round, which falls, fat-wise, somewhere between ground sirloin and ground chuck, is the perfect compromise, resulting in a meat loaf that is neither too dry and compact nor too crumbly and greasy. (The traditional meat loaf blend consists of approximately one pound of beef, ½ pound of pork and ½ pound of veal—proportions that approach ideal.) Whatever meat you use, at whatever fat level, must be freshly ground and full of its natural juices. Several-days-old meat may be perfectly wholesome, but will be compact, hard to mix with the other ingredients and dry.

Ground turkey and chicken are now widely available, though to my palate, the supermarket versions are unsuitable in meat loaf. When using chicken or turkey, I prefer to bone out breast and thigh meat, chill it well and coarsely chop it in the food processor, using short bursts of power.

Not only is such meat fresher, it contains no ground skin, and because the resulting loaf contains actual nuggets of meat, it is less prone to drying. The same process is used for new-age "meat" loaves out of fish or shrimp.

When you use chicken, turkey, seafood or very lean beef, the moisture must come from another source. Ketchup, barbecue sauce or chili sauce, tomato sauce, milk, beef or chicken stock or broth all work well. A bit of heavy cream or evaporated milk will add a luxurious note. Grated cheddar or Monterey Jack cheese is the secret to many a succulent meat loaf. Vegetables, too, can be employed. Onions, carrots, celery, green or red bell peppers—all are frequently used raw or sautéed. Frozen spinach (thawed and partially squeezed out) is an excellent addition, and the cellulose in grated zucchini or grated apple retains moisture while melting into the texture of the loaf and virtually disappearing. Most meat loaves are baked at a relatively low temperature (350 degrees F), which helps; some are even set into a larger pan of hot water—a *bain marie*, or hot water bath—which insulates them from the oven's direct heat and provides a steamy baking environment.

Texture is important, too. A meat loaf should be neither too loose and crumbly, nor too firm and stodgy. A judicious use of some starchy filler or binder is important, and while there can be too much starch, there can also be too little. (Depending on the rest of the ingredients, from $\frac{1}{4}$ to $\frac{1}{3}$ cup filler per pound of meat is about right.) Bread crumbs, seasoned or plain, fresh or dry are typical choices. So are herbed or plain stuffing mixes, crushed crackers (saltines with unsalted tops are my personal choice for best all-round binder), cooked rice or other grains, rolled oats (their texture works especially well in poultry loaves) and corn flakes or corn flake crumbs. Such speciality items as crushed tortilla or potato chips or crumbled corn, rye or pumpernickel breads all do quadruple duty, holding in the juices and tenderizing the loaf while adding subtle taste and stretching the meat a little further.

And then there is flavor. Some sad meat loaves are as plain as baked burgers. Adding pork is one way to improve the taste, and I'm nearly always happier with a loaf that is at least 25 percent pork. Naturally gelatinous ground veal can be added along with the pork, making the loaf both juicier and easier to slice, as well as adding additional flavor. Other flavor-makers are plenty of aromatic vegetables—onions, garlic, celery—preferably sautéed to bring out some of the sweetness, or even well-browned for an extra depth of flavor. Instant soup mixes, full of highly concentrated flavor, have a long and successful history in meat loaf cookery. Mushrooms, fresh herbs, dried herbs (preferably sautéed along with the vegetables), hot peppers, salsa, Worcestershire sauce, hot pepper sauce and soy sauce, used alone or in combination, contribute also. For an extra fillip of flavor (and a great look), top almost any meat loaf with ketchup, chili sauce or barbecue sauce and top that with several strips of bacon.

Be sure to mix the ingredients thoroughly before baking. Unlike hamburgers, meat loaves do not need a light touch to keep them tender. In a meat loaf, the seasonings and binders must be evenly distributed to insure a compact, easy-to-slice loaf that is well seasoned throughout. Meat that is at room temperature will combine more easily than that which is cold. It *is* possible to handle some meat loaf mixtures too much, resulting in a mealy texture, but in general, more meat loaves are under- rather than over-mixed. Stop mixing when all the ingredients appear evenly distributed and you won't go far wrong. On the other hand, there is one meat loaf in this book whose creator insists it be kneaded for a full 5 minutes to achieve the proper texture.

I always use my hands to mix the meat and form the loaves with good, firm pats. If you like your meat loaf as a true loaf, you might like one of those specially designed pans with a perforated liner that lets the fatty juices drip away. I like lots of crisp crust, so I prefer to shape most loaves into a free-form oval about 2½ inches high in a shallow gratin or baking dish that lets maximum browning take place.

After taking pains to ensure a moist loaf, it would be a shame to then overbake it. For maximum control over doneness I recommend using an instant-reading thermometer. Inserted into the center of the loaf, it gives an immediate readout of the internal temperature. All-beef loaves can be eaten when still slightly pink and juicy, at around 145 degrees F. Loaves containing pork or poultry should cook to about 160 degrees F. Seafood loaves are done at about 130 degrees F. Most loaves will continue to cook (and their internal temperature to rise) for about 5 minutes after coming out of the oven.

All meat loaves should rest in their pans on a rack for a short time before they are served. Many of the juices that have cooked out of the loaf will be reabsorbed, so don't discard these juices until just before serving; the result will be a moister, easier-to-slice meat loaf.

Each of the fifty-two meat loaves in this book comes with what I think of as the perfect side dish. These are often of the simple and homey variety (keep in mind we're not talking about pheasant under glass here). Following each pair of recipes you will also find a short section titled Finishing Touches. When you do the kitchen time, what you cook up by way of accompaniments is your business, and these touches are to be consid-

ered my suggestions on completing the menu, nothing more. The same is true of my ideas for dealing with leftovers.

Speaking of leftovers, opinions vary as to what constitutes a normal serving of meat loaf. I have tried to give a range, but if you are dealing with big eaters or are dreaming of leftover meat loaf, consider doubling the recipe or halving your guest list. If warm, fresh and juicy meat loaf is a comfort during troubled times, then knowing there is leftover meat loaf waiting in the fridge is a double comfort.

Chapter One
COAST TO COAST
Recipes for Good Old American Meat Loaves

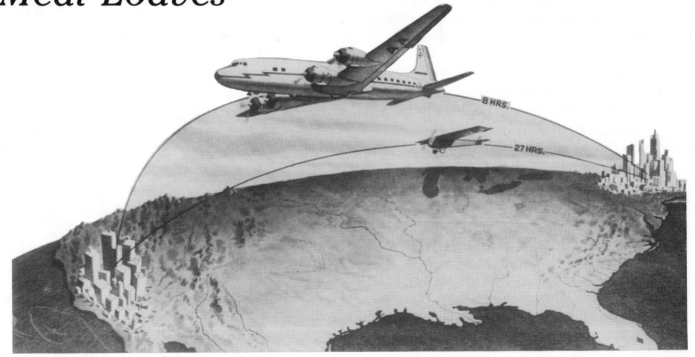

8 HRS.

27 HRS.

This land is your land, this land is my land and from coast to coast, sea to shining sea, the special today is meat loaf, cooked up in dozens of separate but equally delicious ways. At big city suppers and down-on-the-farm dinners, in winter and in summer, from the hills of New England to the streets of Los Angeles, and in restaurants all along the interstate highways, good cooks are stirring up, and eager eaters are anticipating, some form or other of what is surely one of America's favorite dishes. Easy and economical meat loaves also welcome regional embellishments, and if salsa, maple syrup, pineapple or pepperoni are in your pantry, sooner or later you'll think about stirring them into your meat loaf. This isn't experimentation for its own sake, this is how cooking at its most fundamental evolves. The following loaves may not be the ones your mom made while you were growing up, but some mom, or grandma, or crazy cookbook author thinks they taste just like home cooking, and somewhere in America, that's exactly what they are.

Classic Interstate Meat Loaf

Serves 6 to 8

This is The Basic Meat Loaf—all beef, with a touch of green pepper and onion, topped with strips of bacon—instantly recognizable as the truck stop/diner/ hash house American standard. On or off the inter-state, take the advice of one diner cook whose secret I sought and make this meat loaf with "ketchup in and ketchup on" for maximum flavor and moistness.

3 tablespoons unsalted butter
2 cups finely chopped onion
1 medium green bell pepper, finally chopped (about
    ¾ cup)
1 large celery rib, finely chopped
1 teaspoon dried thyme, crumbled
2 pounds ground beef
½ cup rolled oats
⅔ cup ketchup
2 eggs, beaten
2 teaspoons salt
1½ teaspoons freshly ground black pepper
4 slices of bacon, halved crosswise

1. In a medium skillet, melt the butter over medium heat. When it foams, add the onion, bell pepper, celery and thyme. Cover and cook, stirring once or twice, for 10 minutes. Remove from the heat and cool to room temperature.

2. Position a rack in the middle of the oven and preheat the oven to 350 degrees F. In a large bowl, combine the ground beef, the onion mixture, oats, ⅓ cup of the ketchup, the eggs, salt and pepper; mix thoroughly. Spoon the meat mixture into a large, shallow baking dish and shape into a flat loaf about 2 inches high. Smooth the top with the back of a spoon. Spread the remaining ⅓ cup ketchup over the loaf. Arrange the bacon strips, overlapping them slightly, if necessary, on top of the ketchup.

3. Bake the meat loaf for about 1¼ hours, or until an instant-reading thermometer inserted into the center registers 145 degrees F. Let the meat loaf rest on a rack for 10 minutes before slicing. Serve hot.

Creamed Fresh Corn

Serves 6 to 8

For the side of my family that comes from Iowa, and for many other Americans, corn is the symbol of "what to eat." Frequently that corn is canned creamed corn, served as a vegetable or (for ultimate carbohydrate comfort) ladled over mashed potatoes as an easy gravy. When tender sweet corn is in the market (increasingly, with the advent of corn hybrids that stay in peak condition long after picking), this fresh variation is just as comforting, and far tastier, than canned. It's also just right beside a slice of warm, juicy meat loaf.

½ stick (4 tablespoons) unsalted butter
⅓ cup finely chopped onion
4 cups fresh corn kernels and juices, cut and scraped
    from about 16 medium ears
1 cup whipping cream or heavy cream
1½ teaspoons salt
½ teaspoon sugar (optional)
½ teaspoon freshly ground black pepper

1. In a large skillet, melt the butter over low heat. When it foams, add the onion, cover and cook, stirring once or twice, for 10 minutes.

2. Add the corn kernels and juices, cream, salt, sugar and pepper and raise the heat slightly. Partially cover the skillet and cook, stirring often to prevent scorching, until the mixture is thick and the corn is tender, 10 to 12 minutes. *The corn can be prepared to this point up to 1 day ahead. Cover and refrigerate. Rewarm the corn over low heat, stirring often.* Adjust the seasoning. Serve hot.

■ ■ ■

Finishing touches: Serve the meat loaf and creamed corn with fluffy mashed potatoes (use the creamed corn as gravy or just pass plenty of unsalted butter). Accompany the meal with homemade biscuits and drink fresh-brewed iced tea. For dessert, offer a warm fruit cobbler or pie, à la mode if you like.

Leftovers: Wrap sliced meat loaf in foil, warm it in the oven and arrange on crusty bread. Add warmed chili sauce or ketchup to taste.

Apple Scrapple

Serves 8

Scrapple is a frugal, hard-times combination of corn-meal and less-than-prime pig parts—and, it should be admitted, only a distant, though delicious, meat loaf cousin. It's also an acquired taste, one I fortunately acquired years ago. When I'm in scrapple country (Southern Pennsylvania to be exact), I always enjoy a breakfast plateful, napped with maple syrup and accompanied by scrambled eggs. If you're not utilizing everything but the oink from your annual pig butchering, but you still want to sample scrapple, consider the following, rather upscale, company variation.

1½ pounds mildly seasoned bulk pork sausage meat, preferably coarse-ground
1 stick (8 tablespoons) unsalted butter
1 cup finely chopped yellow onion
1 large red apple (such as Red Delicious), cored and cut into ¼-inch dice
1½ tablespoons minced fresh thyme or 1 teaspoon dried, crumbled
1½ tablespoons minced fresh sage or 1 teaspoon ground dried
1 teaspoon freshly ground black pepper
6 cups water
1½ cups yellow cornmeal, preferably stone-ground
2 teaspoons salt
1 cup unbleached all-purpose flour
Maple syrup or honey, warmed

1. Crumble the sausage into a large skillet and set it over medium heat. Cook, stirring and breaking up any large lumps, until the meat is cooked through and lightly browned, 15 to 20 minutes. With a slotted spoon, transfer the sausage to absorbent paper to drain. Discard the fat but do not clean the skillet.

2. Set the skillet over low heat. Add 2 tablespoons of the butter and when it foams, stir in the onion. Cover and cook, stirring once or twice and scraping the pan, for 5 minutes. Stir in the apple, thyme and sage and cook uncovered, stirring once or twice, for 5 minutes. The apple should retain its shape and most of its texture. Return the sausage to the skillet, season with the pepper and mix thoroughly. Set aside.

3. Lightly oil two 9-by-5-by-3-inch loaf pans. In a heavy 4½- to 5-quart pot, slowly whisk the water into the cornmeal. Whisk in the salt. Set the pot over medium heat and bring to a boil, stirring once or twice. Lower the heat, partially cover and simmer, stirring often, until the cornmeal is very thick, about 40 minutes.

4. Stir the sausage mixture into the hot cornmeal, combining well. Divide the mixture while still hot between the prepared pans, smoothing the top. Cool to room temperature, wrap well and refrigerate until firm. *The scrapple can be prepared up to 3 days ahead.*

5. Run a sharp knife between the scrapple and the sides of the loaf pans. Invert each pan onto a cutting board; the scrapple will drop out. Cut each loaf of scrapple into 8 thick slices.

6. In a large skillet, melt the remaining 6 tablespoons butter over medium heat. On a plate, dredge the scrapple slices in the flour, tapping off the excess. Working in batches, fry the scrapple, turning it once, until well browned and crisp, about 4 minutes per side. Serve hot and pass a pitcher of warm maple syrup at the table.

■ ■ ■

Leftovers: Leftover scrapple can be sautéed for another meal, even lunch or supper, or it can be frozen for up to 1 month.

Eggs Scrambled with Toast

Serves 8

Use good-quality, firm, flavorful white or whole wheat bread, several days old. Cubed, toasted and scrambled into the eggs, it becomes partly crunchy, partly custardy, utterly delectable.

4 slices of good-quality sandwich bread, cut ½ inch thick
16 eggs
1 teaspoon salt
½ teaspoon freshly ground black pepper
¾ stick (6 tablespoons) unsalted butter
½ cup finely chopped flat-leaf parsley

1. Preheat the oven to 450 degrees F. With a serrated knife, cut the bread slices into ½-inch cubes; there should be about 4½ cups. Lay the bread cubes in a pan large enough to hold them in a single layer and bake, stirring once or twice, until the bread is crisp and lightly colored, about 15 minutes.

2. In a large bowl, beat the eggs. Whisk in the salt and pepper. In a large skillet, melt the butter over medium heat. Add the bread cubes and toss to coat them lightly with melted butter. Add the eggs and cook, stirring often, for about 7 minutes, or until they are done to your liking. Stir in the parsley and serve immediately.

Firecracker BBQ Chicken Loaf

Serves 8 to 10

My big bang theory of how to eat well on the Fourth of July includes barbecued chicken, lavishly basted with a fiery sauce and cooked up crisp and smoky on a backyard grill. To keep to that general all-American cookout theme while adding a fresh twist, consider this savory chicken loaf for your next Independence Day celebration. And come January, when the firecrackers and fireflies of summer are only a memory, the same meat loaf eaten indoors will recall those days of great backyard eating.

½ stick (4 tablespoons) unsalted butter
2 cups finely chopped onion
½ cup finely chopped celery
1 teaspoon dried thyme leaves, crumbled
1 cup thick and smoky, tomato-based, prepared barbecue sauce
1 tablespoon hot pepper sauce
1 tablespoon Worcestershire sauce
1 tablespoon unsulphured molasses
3 eggs, beaten
2 teaspoons salt
1 teaspoon freshly ground black pepper
3 pounds ground chicken
1 cup corn flake crumbs

1. In a large skillet, melt the butter over medium heat. Add the onion, celery and thyme, cover and cook, stirring once or twice, until soft and lightly colored, 8 to 10 minutes. Remove from the heat and cool to room temperature.

2. Position a rack in the middle of the oven and preheat the oven to 350 degrees F. In a small bowl, whisk together the barbecue sauce, hot pepper sauce, Worcestershire sauce and molasses. Remove ⅓ cup of the barbecue sauce mixture and whisk it into the beaten eggs. Whisk in the salt and pepper.

3. In a large bowl, thoroughly mix together the ground chicken, corn flake crumbs and the egg mixture. Transfer the meat mixture to a shallow baking dish and form it into a flat loaf about 2½ inches high, smoothing the top with the back of a spoon. Spread the top of the loaf evenly with the remaining barbecue sauce mixture.

4. Bake the meat loaf for 1¼ hours, or until an instant-reading thermometer inserted into the center registers 160 degrees F. Let the meat loaf rest on a rack for 10 minutes before slicing. Serve hot.

State Fair Potato and Egg Salad with Sweet Pickles

Serves 8 to 10

This lush salad is a blending of two food memories: one, my mother's mayonnaise-bound potato salad decorated with segments of hard-cooked eggs; and the other, an egg salad thick with sweet pickles, which was the filling of a cherished midnight snack sandwich of mine for years. Here they have merged into one wonderful dish. It has an old-fashioned quality (maybe it's all those now-forbidden eggs!) that makes it perfect for a cookout or a picnic.

4 pounds white- or red-skinned boiling potatoes
    (about 8 large), peeled and cut into 1-inch
    chunks
½ cup sweet pickle juice
1 cup mayonnaise
1 cup sour cream
2 tablespoons Dijon-style mustard
1 teaspoon salt
1 teaspoon freshly ground black pepper
6 hard-cooked eggs, shelled and coarsely chunked
⅔ cup diced red onion
⅔ cup sliced sweet pickles

1. In a large saucepan, cover the potatoes with cold salted water and set over medium heat. Bring to a boil, then lower the heat slightly and cook uncovered, stirring once or twice, until the potatoes are just tender, about 7 minutes. Drain and transfer to a large bowl. Pour the pickle juice over the hot potatoes, stir once or twice and cool to room temperature.

2. In a medium bowl, whisk together the mayonnaise, sour cream, mustard, salt and pepper. Pour the mayonnaise mixture over the potatoes and toss gently. Add the eggs, red onion and sweet pickles and toss again. *The salad can be prepared up to 1 day ahead. Refrigerate, covered, returning the salad to room temperature and tossing it gently just before serving.*

■ ■ ■

Finishing touches: Serve the chicken and potato salad with buttered corn on the cob. Drink lemonade, iced tea or a chilled beer. Serve wedges of ice-cold watermelon for dessert.

Leftovers: Oven warm thin slices of meat loaf wrapped in foil. Arrange them on a hard roll and serve topped with coleslaw.

Millie's Pork and Ham Loaf with Sweet Mustard Glaze

Serves 6 to 8

This simple, Depression-era recipe is from my grandmother Millie's hand-written recipe book. It's the meal my mother always makes for the first dinner when I'm home for a visit. You should expect to order the ground pork and to chop the ham yourself in a food processor.

1 pound firm and smoky baked ham, trimmed of any
    fat and tough rind and cut into chunks
1½ pounds ground pork
1 cup finely crushed saltine crackers (about 2½
    ounces)
1 cup milk
2 eggs, beaten
1 teaspoon freshly ground black pepper
Sweet Mustard Glaze (recipe follows)

1. Position a rack in the lower third of the oven and preheat the oven to 350 degrees F. In a food processor, finely chop the ham. In a large bowl, stir together the ham and pork. Add the cracker crumbs, milk, eggs and pepper and mix thoroughly. Transfer the meat mixture to a shallow baking dish and form it into a flat loaf about 2½ inches thick. With the back of a knife, press a diamond crosshatch pattern about ½ inch deep into the upper surface of the loaf.

2. Bake the loaf for 30 minutes. Spread one-third of the mustard glaze over the loaf and bake for 15 minutes. Spread half of the remaining glaze over the loaf and bake for 15 minutes. Spread the last of the glaze over the loaf and bake for another 15 to 20 minutes, or until the loaf is glazed and brown and an instant-reading thermometer inserted in the center reads 165 degrees F.

3. Cool for 5 minutes and transfer the loaf to a serving platter. Let rest for another 5 minutes before cutting. Serve hot.

Sweet Mustard Glaze

Makes about 1 cup

1 cup packed light brown sugar
⅓ cup cider vinegar
⅓ cup water
¼ cup Dijon-style mustard

In a small, nonreactive saucepan, whisk together the brown sugar, vinegar, water and mustard. Bring to a boil, lower the heat and simmer uncovered, stirring once or twice, for 20 minutes. Cool to room temperature. *The glaze can be prepared several days ahead. Store it, covered, at room temperature.*

Mashed Potato Cakes

Serves 6 to 8

The idea for this dish also comes from Millie's recipe book. Originally devised as a frugal way to use up leftover mashed potatoes, these cakes are golden and crusty on the outside, creamy and hot within—and good enough to make on purpose. Here is my adaptation, utilizing my mother's suggestion that a bit of added onion won't hurt a thing.

4 pounds russet baking potatoes (7 to 8 large), peeled and chunked
1¼ sticks (10 tablespoons) unsalted butter
6 green onions, trimmed and sliced (about ¾ cup)
¼ cup milk
2 teaspoons salt
1 teaspoon freshly ground black pepper
3 eggs, beaten
¼ cup unbleached all-purpose flour

1. In a large pot, cover the potatoes with cold salted water and set over medium heat. Bring the water to a boil, then lower the heat slightly and cook, stirring once or twice, until the potatoes are very tender, about 25 minutes.

2. Meanwhile, in a small skillet, melt 4 tablespoons of the butter over medium-low heat. When it foams, stir in the green onions and cook for 2 minutes, or until the onions are slightly wilted. Remove from the heat.

3. Drain the potatoes and force them through the medium disk of a food mill or mash them by hand; do not use a food processor. Return the potatoes to their pan and set over low heat. Stir the potatoes constantly for 3 minutes. Stir in the milk and the green onions with their butter. Beat the potatoes for a minute or two, until they are fluffy. Season with the salt and pepper. Cool the potatoes to room temperature and whisk in the beaten eggs and the flour. *The recipe can be prepared to this point up to 1 day ahead. Cover and refrigerate, returning the potatoes to room temperature before proceeding.*

4. In each of 2 large skillets, or in 1 large skillet working in batches, melt 3 tablespoons of the butter over medium heat. Using a ⅓-cup measure (or an ice cream scooper of about that capacity), portion the potato mixture, dropping each into the hot butter in the skillets. With a fork flatten the potato mixture into 4-inch rounds about ¾ inch thick. Fry, carefully turning each potato cake once, until golden brown, 4 to 5 minutes per side. Transfer to a warmed platter until all of the cakes are fried. Serve hot.

■ ■ ■

Finishing touches: Serve the ham loaf and potato cakes with Well-Cheddared Broccoli (page 79) or buttered brussels sprouts. At Millie's table there would be bread with plenty of butter. An amber ale or a dark beer would be good to drink with the sweet-and-salty ham loaf.

Leftovers: Wrap thin slices of the ham loaf in foil and heat in the oven. Arrange on rye or pumpernickel bread and spread with honey or Dijon mustard.

Hazel's Pressed Chicken Loaf

Serves 6 to 8

Here is a recipe from my other grandmother, a great cook and, as the widowed mother of four running a dairy almost single-handedly, by necessity a frugal cook as well. This simple loaf was devised to make a meal out of a tough old chicken—rooster or brood hen—gone past its prime. The lengthy cooking needed to tenderize the critter unfortunately rendered the meat rather dry, a condition disguised by chopping the meat and binding it and its broth with absorbent cracker crumbs. I have enriched the broth somewhat, since today's supermarket chickens don't simmer half so long as Hazel's yard birds, but the taste remains the same—a taste that is, according to my brutally honest mother, "rather *blah*—but when you know pressed chicken is going to be on the menu, you just can't stop thinking about it."

1 whole (about 4½ pounds) chicken, including the giblets but not the liver
1 large can (46 ounces) chicken broth
1 cup finely chopped onion
1 medium carrot, peeled and chopped
1 celery rib, chopped
2 bay leaves
1 cup saltine cracker crumbs
1 teaspoon salt
¾ teaspoon freshly ground black pepper
Mayonnaise or salad dressing, as accompaniment

1. In a 5-quart pot, set the chicken breast side-up. Pour the broth over the chicken. Add the giblets, onion, carrot, celery, bay leaves and as much additional water as is needed to just cover the bird.

2. Set over medium heat and bring to a simmer. Partially cover the pan and cook, turning the chicken over at about the halfway point, for about 45 minutes, or until the meat is just tender. Remove the pan from the heat and let the chicken cool to room temperature in the poaching liquid.

3. Remove the chicken from the pot. Strain and degrease the poaching liquid. Measure out 1½ cups, reserving the remainder of the broth for another use. Remove the skin from the chicken and pick the meat from the bones. In a food processor, using short bursts of power, finely chop the meat.

4. In a large bowl, combine the chopped chicken meat, reserved 1½ cups broth, cracker crumbs, salt and pepper. Lightly oil an 8-by-4-by-2½-inch loaf pan. Firmly pack the chicken mixture into the loaf pan. Cover tightly and refrigerate until firm, preferably overnight.

5. Invert the loaf pan onto a cutting board. If necessary, dip a cloth into hot water, wring it out and press it onto the bottom of the pan to release the loaf. Cut the loaf into thick slices and serve cold or at room temperature, accompanied by mayonnaise or salad dressing.

Church Supper Salad

Serves 6 to 8

This is my version of the popular "seven-layer salad." Sealed into its serving dish by a thick frosting of mayonnaise-based dressing, the salad is favored by busy cooks for its ability to wait overnight in the refrigerator before being taken along to a church supper or other social event. It's just as good without the wait, of course, tossed and served upon completion, and I have eliminated that step while otherwise sticking to a rather unorthodox list of ingredients that somehow manages to be absolutely delicious. Blue cheese can be substituted for the cheddar—just use a little less.

½ pound sliced bacon
1 cup mayonnaise
1 cup salad dressing, such as Miracle Whip
½ cup buttermilk
1 tablespoon Dijon-style mustard
2 teaspoons hot pepper sauce
16 cups sturdy salad greens, such as romaine lettuce
    and curly-leaf spinach, torn into bite-size
    pieces
10 ounces white mushrooms, sliced
1 package (10 ounces) frozen peas, thawed and
    drained
8 ounces cheddar cheese, grated (about 2 cups)
1 small red onion, sliced into thin rings

1. Lay the bacon slices in a cold skillet, set the skillet over medium heat and cook, turning the slices, until they are crisp, 8 to 10 minutes. Drain the bacon on absorbent paper and when it is cool, coarsely chop it.

2. In a medium bowl, whisk together the mayonnaise, salad dressing, buttermilk, mustard and hot pepper sauce.

3. In a large bowl, combine the salad greens, mushrooms and mayonnaise mixture and toss well. Add the bacon, peas, half of the grated cheese and the red onion rings and toss again. Transfer the salad to a bowl or platter, sprinkle with the remaining cheese and serve.

■ ■ ■

Finishing touches: Serve the pressed chicken and salad with sliced tomatoes. Accompany the meal with hot rolls and sweet butter and drink fresh lemonade. Dessert should be a tall, homemade cake—angel food, devil's food or German chocolate.

Leftovers: Leftover pressed chicken is always (and I mean always) enjoyed on a sandwich of soft white bread liberally spread with mayonnaise or Miracle Whip with a thin layer of iceberg lettuce.

New England Corned Beef Loaf

Serves 6 to 8

This savory loaf will be best if made with corned beef that is left over from a boiled dinner, or any other meal in which a whole corned brisket has been gently simmered into succulence. Fully cooked, sliced corned beef, available in some supermarkets, can be substituted, but do not use processed, sliced corned beef sandwich meats.

¾ pound trimmed cooked corned beef
1½ pounds ground beef
1 cup fine, dry bread crumbs
1 cup milk
½ cup finely chopped onion
2 eggs, beaten
1 teaspoon salt
½ teaspoon freshly ground black pepper
¼ cup maple syrup
3 tablespoons Dijon-style mustard

1. Cut the corned beef into small chunks and, in a food processor, using short bursts of power, finely chop the meat.

2. Position a rack in the middle of the oven and preheat the oven to 350 degrees F. In a large bowl, combine the corned beef, ground beef, bread crumbs, milk, onion, eggs, salt and pepper and mix thoroughly. Transfer the meat mixture to a 9-by-5-by-3-inch loaf pan, mounding it slightly.

3. Bake the meat loaf for 30 minutes. In a small bowl, stir together the maple syrup and mustard. Spread half of the maple mixture over the top of the loaf and bake it 20 minutes. Spread the remaining maple mixture over the loaf and bake it 20 minutes longer, or until an instant-reading thermometer inserted into the center of the loaf registers 145 degrees F. Let rest for 10 minutes before slicing. Serve hot.

Harvard Beets

Serves 6 to 8

These crimson-sauced, sweet-and-sour beets are said to have been inspired by the color of the football jerseys at Harvard, but there is no hard evidence backing up the tale. Easier to prove is their compatibility with the slightly salty and spicy taste of corned beef. Because I like beets that look like beets, I call for medium-size, whole beets, but diced or sliced beets can be substituted. The last minute addition of a bit of butter is optional, but it adds a rich note and extra gloss to the sauce.

1/3 cup red wine vinegar
2 tablespoons cornstarch
2 cans (16 ounces each) medium whole beets, drained, juices reserved (about 1 2/3 cups)
1/4 cup sugar
1/2 teaspoon salt
1/2 teaspoon freshly ground black pepper
1 tablespoon unsalted butter

1. In a small bowl, gradually stir the vinegar into the cornstarch. In a medium nonreactive saucepan, set the beet juices over medium heat. Whisk in the cornstarch mixture and the sugar, salt and pepper. Bring to a simmer, stirring often, and cook for about 3 minutes, or until the sauce thickens slightly and becomes translucent.

2. Stir in the beets and cook for another 2 to 3 minutes, or until the sauce is thick and the beets are heated through. *The recipe can be prepared to this point several hours in advance. Warm over low heat, stirring often.* Stir in the butter and serve hot.

■ ■ ■

Finishing touches: Lemon-Parsley New Potatoes (page 119) would be a fine accompaniment to the meat loaf, but so would almost any other potato preparation. Serve steamed Boston brown bread (or any good, whole grain bread) and drink a regional ale like Samuel Adams. The cornmeal and molasses sweet known as Indian pudding would be a fine dessert (though a lot of work); you may offer good ice cream instead.

Leftovers: Getting a sandwich out of a leftover meat loaf made from leftover corned beef is real New England frugality. Serve it on brown bread, with a generous schmear of honey mustard.

Salsa-topped Beef and Black Bean Loaf

Serves 6 to 8

This beef loaf, made with enchilada sauce, crushed tortilla chips and smoky black beans, sizzles with Cal-Mex flavor (hot salsa, also). Perhaps such loaves get cooked up in Latin kitchens, and perhaps this is only a fantasy of mine. Either way, two cultures cross-pollinate, and the winner is the lucky diner confronted with a plate of this zesty treat.

¼ cup olive oil
2 cups finely chopped onions
3 garlic cloves, minced
2 teaspoons ground cumin
2 teaspoons dried oregano, crumbled
1 teaspoon crushed hot red pepper
1 can (10 ounces) hot enchilada sauce
1½ teaspoons salt
1 teaspoon freshly ground black pepper
2 pounds ground beef
2 eggs, beaten
1 cup finely crushed, unspiced corn tortilla chips
1 can (16 ounces) black beans, rinsed and drained
¾ cup tomato-based, bottled hot salsa

1. In a large skillet, warm the olive oil over medium heat. Add the onions, garlic, cumin, oregano and crushed hot pepper, cover and cook, stirring once or twice, until the onions are lightly colored, 8 to 10 minutes. Stir in the enchilada sauce, salt and pepper and cook uncovered, stirring once or twice, for 5 minutes. Remove from the heat and cool to room temperature.

2. Position a rack in the middle of the oven and preheat the oven to 350 degrees F. In a large bowl, combine the ground beef, enchilada sauce mixture, eggs, crushed tortilla chips and black beans and mix thoroughly. Transfer the meat mixture to a shallow baking dish and form it into a flat loaf about 2½ inches thick; smooth the top with the back of a spoon. Spread the salsa evenly over the meat loaf.

3. Bake for 1¼ hours, or until an instant-reading thermometer inserted into the center of the loaf registers 145 degrees F. Let the meat loaf rest on a rack for 10 minutes before slicing. Serve hot.

Tomato, Avocado and Lettuce Salad

Serves 6 to 8

This colorful, vinegar-and-oil-dressed salad is a fork-eaten cousin of the familiar Mexican dip, guacamole. Use only pear-shaped, black-skinned Haas avocados and the ripest, juiciest tomatoes you can locate. Pungent, perishable cilantro gives the salad an authentic flavor, but if it is unavailable, the herb can be omitted.

4 medium tomatoes (about 2 pounds), trimmed and
    cut into 1-inch chunks
¼ cup red wine vinegar
1 teaspoon salt
¼ cup olive oil
½ cup minced cilantro
1 teaspoon freshly ground black pepper
3 buttery ripe, black-skinned avocados, pitted, peeled
    and cut into 1-inch chunks
Tender inner leaves of 2 heads of romaine lettuce,
    separated, rinsed and patted dry

1. In a large mixing bowl, stir together the tomatoes, vinegar and salt. Let stand at room temperature, stirring once or twice, for 30 minutes.

2. Stir in the olive oil, cilantro and pepper. Gently stir in the avocados. Arrange the lettuce leaves on salad plates and divide the tomato mixture atop the lettuce leaves. Spoon any remaining dressing from the bowl evenly over the salads and serve immediately.

Finishing touches: Accompany the meat loaf and salad with hot buttered corn bread. Drink fresh limeade or chilled beer. For dessert, arrange fresh fruit on plates, top with a scoop of purchased sorbet of your choice and drizzle each scoop with 1 tablespoon of gold tequila.

Leftovers: Top slices of meat loaf with slices of jalapeño Jack cheese. Wrap each slice in a flour tortilla and then in foil and oven warm until the meat loaf is hot and the cheese is melted. Serve these "burritos" with additional salsa, shredded lettuce and chopped tomato.

Pineapple Luau Loaf

Serves 6 to 8

Pork, pineapple and ginger combine to excellent effect, giving this meat loaf a vaguely tropical flavor. It's hardly authentic Hawaiian cuisine (for that you need mahimahi, banana leaves, poi, marinated raw fish salads and other Pacific Rim edibles), but residents of the fiftieth state, as well as meat loaf lovers everywhere, will nevertheless recognize it as a particularly successful meat loaf.

½ stick (4 tablespoons) unsalted butter
1 cup finely chopped onion
1 large, heavy red bell pepper, finely chopped
3 garlic cloves, minced
1 tablespoon grated fresh ginger
2 pounds ground pork
½ cup fine, dry bread crumbs
2 eggs, beaten
2 tablespoons soy sauce
1 teaspoon salt
1 teaspoon freshly ground black pepper
1 small can (8 ounces) crushed pineapple, drained
¼ cup tomato sauce
2 tablespoons packed light brown sugar
1 tablespoon Dijon-style mustard

1. In a large skillet, melt the butter over medium heat. When it foams, add the onion, bell pepper, garlic and ginger, cover and cook, stirring once or twice, until the onion is lightly colored, 8 to 10 minutes. Remove from the heat and cool to room temperature.

2. Position a rack in the middle of the oven and preheat the oven to 350 degrees F. In a large bowl, combine the ground pork, onion-red pepper mixture, bread crumbs, eggs, 1 tablespoon of the soy sauce, the salt and the pepper and mix thoroughly. Transfer the meat mixture to a 9-by-5-by-3-inch loaf pan and mound it slightly. In a small bowl, mix together the pineapple, tomato sauce, brown sugar, mustard and remaining 1 tablespoon soy sauce. Spread the mixture evenly over the meat loaf.

3. Bake the meat loaf for about 1½ hours, or until an instant-reading thermometer, inserted into the center of the loaf registers 160 degrees F. Let the meat loaf rest on a rack for 10 minutes before slicing. Serve hot.

Macadamia Sugar Snap Peas

Serves 6 to 8

The entire pod of the tender, sweet sugar snap pea is edible, making it a crunchy delight to eat, especially when compared to the more familiar (and similarly flavored) snow pea. Combined with one of Hawaii's finest products—the macadamia nut—and a bit of soy sauce and butter, sugar snaps make a fine accompaniment to the pineapple-topped meat loaf.

1½ pounds sugar snap peas, tipped and stringed if necessary
½ stick (4 tablespoons) unsalted butter
½ cup coarsely chopped macadamia nuts
2 teaspoons soy sauce
½ teaspoon freshly ground black pepper

1. Bring a large pot of salted water to a boil. Add the sugar snap peas and cook, stirring once or twice, until the peas are just tender, about 4 minutes. Drain into a colander and rinse under cold running water; drain well. *The sugar snap peas can be prepared up to 1 day ahead. Wrap well and refrigerate.*

2. In a large skillet, melt the butter over medium heat. When it foams, add the macadamia nuts and cook, stirring once or twice, until the nuts are lightly colored, about 5 minutes. Add the sugar snap peas, raise the heat slightly and cook, stirring and tossing often, until the sugar snaps are heated through, about 5 minutes. Remove the skillet from the heat, stir in the soy sauce and pepper. Serve hot.

■ ■ ■

Finishing touches: Accompany the meat loaf and sugar snap peas with steamed white rice, for the Asian touch, or Potatoes and Corn au Gratin (page 133), for a more American approach. Either beer or chilled fresh fruit juice would be a good beverage choice, and for dessert, consider a home-baked coconut cream pie.

Leftovers: Cube any leftover meat loaf, combine it with leftover rice, sliced green onions and chunks of fresh pineapple. Add bottled sesame-soy or poppy seed dressing and toss; serve atop salad greens.

Little Italy Pepperoni-Mushroom Pizza Loaf

Serves 6 to 8

I've never liked the idea of pizza topped with ground beef, but a ground beef loaf that tastes like pizza is a very good idea, indeed. The mushrooms and mozzarella go inside the loaf; the pepperoni slices go on top, where they bake up crisp. It is at least as good as anything you'll find in Little Italy.

¼ cup olive oil
2 cups finely chopped onions
4 garlic cloves, minced
1 tablespoon dried oregano, crumbled
½ teaspoon crushed hot red pepper
10 ounces fresh mushrooms, coarsely chopped
2 teaspoons salt
1 cup pizza sauce, such as Ragu
2½ pounds ground beef
3 eggs, beaten
½ cup fine, dry bread crumbs
1 teaspoon freshly ground black pepper
½ pound mozzarella cheese, cut into ½-inch cubes
3 ounces sliced pepperoni

1. In a large skillet, warm the olive oil over medium heat. Add the onions, garlic, oregano and crushed hot pepper, cover and cook, stirring once or twice, for 10 minutes. Add the mushrooms and 1 teaspoon of the salt, raise the heat to medium-high and cook uncovered, tossing and stirring the mushrooms often, until they render their juices and are tender, about 10 minutes. Stir in ½ cup of the pizza sauce, remove from the heat and cool to room temperature.

2. Position a rack in the middle of the oven and preheat the oven to 350 degrees F. In a large bowl, combine the ground beef, the mushroom mixture, eggs, bread crumbs, remaining 1 teaspoon salt and the black pepper and mix thoroughly. Add the cubes of mozzarella and mix until evenly distributed. Transfer the meat mixture to a shallow baking dish and shape it into a flat loaf about 2½ inches thick. Smooth the top of the loaf with the back of a spoon. Spread the remaining ½ cup pizza sauce evenly over the loaf. Lay the pepperoni slices evenly over the pizza sauce, overlapping them if necessary and using them all.

3. Bake the meat loaf for about 1¼ hours, pouring off accumulated pan juices as necessary, or until an instant-reading thermometer inserted into the center registers 145 degrees F. Let stand for 10 minutes before slicing. Serve hot.

Pasta Bow Ties with Zucchini and Roasted Red Peppers

Serves 6 to 8

Pasta with your pizza may be the ultimate indulgence, Italian style. Freshly roasted red bell peppers will make better eating, but in a pinch, good-quality peppers from a jar can be substituted, as can a different short pasta shape, such as fusilli or penne. Without the meat loaf (but why?) this makes a colorful light supper dish for four diners.

2 medium, heavy red bell peppers
1 pound farfalle (dried pasta bow ties), preferably imported
3 teaspoons salt
¼ cup olive oil
4 medium zucchini (about 1½ pounds), scrubbed, halved lengthwise and cut crosswise ½ inch thick
8 garlic cloves, coarsely chopped
½ teaspoon crushed hot red pepper
1 cup chicken stock or canned broth
1 cup grated Parmesan cheese, plus additional cheese for the table

1. In the open flame of a gas burner or under a preheated electric broiler, roast the peppers, turning them, until the peels are blackened. Steam the peppers in a closed paper bag until cool. Rub away the burnt peel, stem and core the peppers and cut into ¼-inch dice.

2. Bring a large pot of water to a boil. Stir in the pasta and 2 teaspoons of the salt. Cook until just tender, about 9 minutes after the water returns to the boil. Drain thoroughly.

3. Meanwhile, in a large skillet, warm the olive oil over medium heat. Add the zucchini, garlic and crushed hot pepper and cook, tossing and stirring often, until the garlic and zucchini are lightly browned, about 7 minutes. Stir in the chopped, roasted peppers and the remaining 1 teaspoon salt and cook, stirring, for 1 minute. Stir in the drained pasta and the chicken broth and cook over high heat, stirring often, until the pasta has absorbed most of the liquid, about 3 minutes. Stir in 1 cup Parmesan cheese and toss well. Serve hot, passing additional grated cheese at the table, if desired.

■ ■ ■

Finishing touches: Serve the meat loaf and pasta with garlic bread, and follow with a balsamic vinegar-dressed green salad. Accompany the meal with hot garlic bread and drink Chianti or a zinfandel from California. For dessert, serve cheesecake garnished with fresh strawberries or purchased spumoni.

Leftovers: Lay thin slices of meat loaf on a soft Italian roll and top with thin slices of mozzarella or provolone cheese. Wrap in foil and bake in the oven until the meat loaf is hot and the cheese is melted.

Pork Loaf with Apples and Cheese

Serves 6 to 8

Here cheese and apples subtly merge with pork to create an indescribably savory and delicious meat loaf. The apples add flavor and moisture, not sweetness, while the piquant glaze contributes the right touch of contrast. For best eye appeal, use red (beet-flavored) horseradish.

½ stick (4 tablespoons) unsalted butter
2 medium tart apples, such as McIntosh, cored and grated (about 2 cups)
1½ cups finely chopped onions
2 pounds ground pork
4 ounces medium-sharp cheddar cheese, grated (about 1 cup)
¾ cup saltine cracker crumbs
2 eggs, beaten
1½ teaspoons salt
1 teaspoon freshly ground black pepper
½ cup apple jelly
¼ cup prepared horseradish, preferably red

1. In a large skillet, melt the butter over medium heat. When it foams, stir in the apples and onions, cover and cook, stirring once or twice, for 5 minutes. Uncover the skillet and cook, stirring once or twice, until tender and lightly colored, 4 to 5 minutes more. Remove from the heat and cool to room temperature.

2. Position a rack in the middle of the oven and preheat the oven to 350 degrees F. In a large bowl, combine the ground pork with the apple-onion mixture, grated cheese, cracker crumbs, eggs, salt and pepper and blend well. Transfer the mixture to a shallow baking dish and shape into a loaf about 2½ inches high; smooth the top of the loaf with the back of a spoon.

3. Bake the meat loaf for 30 minutes. In a small bowl, stir together the apple jelly and horseradish. Spread about one-third of the jelly mixture over the loaf and bake for 20 minutes. Spread the loaf with half of the remaining jelly mixture and bake for 20 minutes longer. Spread the remaining jelly mixture over the loaf and bake for another 15 to 20 minutes, or until an instant-reading thermometer inserted into the center of the loaf registers 160 degrees F. Let the meat loaf stand on a rack for 10 minutes before slicing. Serve hot.

Baked Maple-Rum Squash

Serves 8

Squash can stand a little sweetening, especially when that sweetener is genuine maple syrup, tempered with a splash of dark rum. If you wish, drop an extra pat of butter into each squash half just before serving.

4 small acorn squash (about 1 pound each)
½ stick (4 tablespoons) unsalted butter
½ cup maple syrup
½ cup dark rum
¾ teaspoon salt
½ teaspoon freshly ground black pepper

1. Cut each squash lengthwise in half and scrape out the seeds. Set the squash halves, cut sides-up, on a jelly roll sheet pan, trimming the bottoms if necessary so that the halves sit level.

2. Position a rack in the middle of the oven and preheat the oven to 350 degrees F. Add ½ tablespoon butter and 1 tablespoon each maple syrup and dark rum to the cavity of each squash half. Season evenly with the salt and pepper.

3. Bake for about 50 minutes, basting every 10 minutes or so with the melted butter mixture from the cavities. The squash are done when a fork pierces the thickest edge easily. Let stand for 5 minutes before serving. Serve hot.

■ ■ ■

Finishing touches: Serve this loaf and the squash with Potatoes and Corn au Gratin (page 133). Accompany the meal with a rustic, seeded rye bread loaf and drink an amber beer, such as New Amsterdam. For dessert, bake a simple pear dessert, such as a brown Betty or a crisp, and serve it warm, with a dollop of unsweetened whipped cream.

Leftovers: This meat loaf is good cold, sliced thin, in a sandwich of seeded rye bread spread with a mixture of apple butter and horseradish.

Germantown Meat Loaf with Sauerkraut, Horseradish and Dill

Serves 6 to 8

This loaf is from a mythical, not an actual, Germantown, a place where the hearty eating and rich, winter flavors of middle European cooking persist in such modern American fare as meat loaf. Though there are a lot of aggressively flavored ingredients in the recipe, they are all used in moderation, resulting in a well-balanced but intensely satisfying dish.

½ stick (4 tablespoons) unsalted butter
1½ cups finely chopped onions
2½ teaspoons dried dill weed, crumbled
8 ounces refrigerated fresh—not canned—sauerkraut, drained and chopped
1 pound ground beef
½ pound ground pork
½ pound ground veal
⅔ cup fresh crumbs from seeded rye or pumpernickel bread
2 eggs, beaten
2 tablespoons Dijon-style mustard
2 tablespoons prepared white horseradish
1½ teaspoons salt
1 teaspoon freshly ground black pepper
1 can (8 ounces) tomato sauce
¼ cup packed dark brown sugar

1. In a large nonreactive skillet, melt the butter over medium heat. When it foams, stir in the onions and dill, cover and cook, stirring once or twice, for 5 minutes. Stir in the sauerkraut, cover and cook, stirring once or twice, for another 5 minutes, or until the onions are tender and lightly colored. Remove from the heat and cool to room temperature.

2. Position a rack in the middle of the oven and preheat the oven to 350 degrees F. In a large bowl, combine the ground beef, pork and veal with the onion mixture, bread crumbs, eggs, mustard, horseradish, salt and pepper and blend well. Transfer the mixture to a 9-by-5-by-3-inch loaf pan, mounding it slightly and smoothing the top of the loaf with the back of a spoon. In a small bowl, whisk together the tomato sauce and brown sugar. Pour the sweetened tomato sauce over the loaf.

3. Bake for about 1½ hours, or until an instant-reading thermometer inserted into the center of the loaf registers 160 degrees F. Let the meat loaf stand on a rack for 10 minutes before slicing. Serve hot.

Apple-Pear Sauce

Serves 6 to 8

Apple sauces are as individual as cooks, so I stress that this is the one I like—a smooth sauce, combining apples with pears, sweetened with a bit of maple syrup. If you prefer things chunky, or like the peels left on and in, or if you want a different sweetener or a handful of raisins, feel free to adapt this easy recipe accordingly. Make it a day ahead so the flavors can mellow, and serve it cold.

2½ pounds tart apples (about 7), peeled, cored and chunked
2½ pounds ripe, juicy pears (6 or 7), peeled, cored and chunked
¾ cup genuine maple syrup
1 cinnamon stick, 2 to 3 inches long
3 tablespoons fresh lemon juice

1. In a large nonreactive saucepan, combine the apples, pears, maple syrup, cinnamon stick and lemon juice. Bring to a simmer over medium heat and cook uncovered, stirring occasionally, until the fruit is very tender, about 20 minutes. Remove from the heat and cool slightly. Discard the cinnamon stick.

2. Force the fruit mixture through the medium disk of a food mill or puree in a food processor. Cool the sauce to room temperature, cover and refrigerate until cold, preferably overnight. *The apple-pear sauce can be prepared up to 3 days ahead and refrigerated, or frozen for up to 3 months.*

3. Before serving, adjust the seasoning, adding additional maple syrup or lemon juice to taste.

■ ■ ■

Finishing touches: Serve the meat loaf and apple-pear sauce with The Mashed Potatoes (page 75) and a buttered green vegetable like brussels sprouts. Accompany the meat with black or seeded rye bread and drink a German beer, such as Beck's. For dessert, offer a plate of homemade butter cookies and drink coffee topped with whipped cream.

Leftovers: Make sandwiches of this meat loaf and Swiss cheese, sliced thin, piled onto rye or pumpernickel bread and generously spread with honey mustard.

Chapter Two

A VIEW FROM ABROAD

Recipes with International Flavor

Meat loaf is too good and too big for America alone. Ground up meat has been the frugal, sensible ingredient in mankind's meals ever since the first caveman bagged the first mastodon (talk about leftovers). If the U.S. has made the most of meat loaf, that's just because our food enthusiasms are, like everything else around here, larger than life. Early (but not prehistoric) meat loaves were no doubt plain janes, reflecting the humble status of the main ingredient. We've gathered here to praise the meat loaf, but let's not forget that ground meat is at bottom a clever way of tenderizing scraps too scrappy to enjoy on their own. American meat loaf recipes were recorded as long ago as the turn of the century, and we can assume few if any contained Dijon mustard, curry powder, mango chutney or teriyaki glaze. As the world has shrunk, however, and as the American palate has shaken off its doldrums, such alien oddities as fresh ginger, bulgur wheat and black Greek olives have come to seem commonplace, and only the most curmudgeonly of meat loaf makers will begrudge the following admittedly fanciful international meat loaf variations, a veritable United Nations of good and zesty eating.

Pretty Much Pâté

Serves 8 to 10

It's trite (but true) that pâtés and meat loaves are close culinary cousins, and despite the French name and the premium ingredients, the former is not much harder to make than the latter. To bridge the two traditions (and perhaps to inspire you to take up pâté-making in earnest one day), here's my pâté-like meat loaf. The technique is simple, but the ingredients combine to produce something very much like the genuine, French thing. I like it best served cool, with a tangy charcuterie salad or two, but it can also be served hot, with Sweet and Sour Red Cabbage (page 63) and Potato and Celery Root Gratin (page 59).

½ stick (4 tablespoons) unsalted butter
1 cup finely chopped onion
1 large leek (white part only), cleaned and finely chopped
3 shallots, minced
4 garlic cloves, minced
1 tablespoon dried thyme leaves, crumbled
3 bay leaves
½ teaspoon freshly grated nutmeg
1 pound ground beef
1 pound ground veal
1 pound ground pork
3 eggs, beaten

½ cup fine, dry bread crumbs
½ cup finely chopped flat-leaf parsley
1 tablespoon salt
1½ teaspoons freshly ground black pepper
½ pound chicken livers, trimmed and cut into ½-inch chunks

1. In a medium skillet, melt the butter over medium heat. Add the onion, leek, shallots, garlic, thyme, bay leaves and nutmeg. Cover and cook, stirring once or twice, for 10 minutes. Remove from the heat, discard the bay leaves and cool to room temperature.

2. Position a rack in the middle of the oven and preheat the oven to 350 degrees F. In a large bowl, combine the ground beef, veal and pork, the onion mixture, eggs, bread crumbs, parsley, salt and pepper and mix thoroughly. Spread about half of the meat mixture in a 1-inch-thick loaf shape in a shallow baking dish. Arrange the chicken livers over the meat layer, leaving a 1-inch border all around. Spread the remaining meat mixture over the chicken livers, press the edges to seal and form gently into a flat loaf; smooth the top with the back of a spoon.

3. Bake for about 1 hour and 20 minutes, or until an instant-reading thermometer inserted into the center of the loaf registers 160 degrees F. Let the loaf rest on a rack for 10 minutes before slicing, if serving hot, or cool the loaf completely to room temperature, if serving cool. *The meat loaf can be baked up to 1 day ahead. Wrap well and refrigerate, returning it to room temperature before slicing and serving.*

Charcuterie Coleslaw

Serves 8 to 10

Charcuteries are those French food establishments specializing in pâtés, sausages, other cooked meaty fare and the appropriate accompaniments. There you might find a tangy, mustardy celeriac salad to serve alongside your pâté, and, spooned out of a cool crock, the tiny sour pickles known as cornichons. In this country, coleslaw is a likelier partner to cold meat loaf, but there's no reason not to stir in a few, charcuterie-type ingredients, particularly when the results are so compatible with the main course. Some supermarkets stock cornichons, or look for them at a good cheese shop.

1½ cups mayonnaise
1½ cups sour cream
¼ cup coarsely grained Dijon-style mustard
¼ cup red wine vinegar
2 tablespoons sugar (optional)
1 teaspoon salt
1 teaspoon freshly ground black pepper
1 large cabbage (3 pounds), trimmed, cored and
    shredded (about 10 cups)
¾ cup sliced cornichons
½ cup finely chopped flat-leaf parsley

1. In a large bowl, whisk together the mayonnaise, sour cream, mustard, vinegar, sugar, salt and pepper. Add the cabbage and toss to mix thoroughly. Stir in the cornichons. *The coleslaw can be prepared to this point 1 day ahead. Cover and refrigerate.*

2. Just before serving, stir in the parsley. Toss well and adjust the seasoning.

■ ■ ■

Finishing touches: Serve the meat loaf and coleslaw with a vinaigrette-dressed potato salad and a green salad garnished with crumbled Roquefort. Accompany the meal with crusty bread and drink either a dry pink wine (like Rosé d'Anjou) or a chilled beer. Dessert might be purchased French pastries or fresh fruit and nuts in the shell.

Leftovers: Make a sandwich of leftover pâté and coleslaw, piled high on slices of hearty pumpernickel bread.

Cold Veal Loaf with Tuna Mayonnaise

Serves 8 to 10

Vitello tonnato, the Italian dish of cold braised veal coated with a luscious tuna mayonnaise, is one of the world's great dishes. Considerably less work, but no less delicious and intriguing, is this meat loaf variation. Perfect on a hot summer's day and ideal on a picnic, this is about as elegant as it's possible for a meat loaf to get. (The veal loaf can also be served hot, accompanied by the Tomato-Olive Sauce on page 46 in place of the mayonnaise.)

¼ cup olive oil
2 cups finely chopped onions
3 garlic cloves, minced
1 teaspoon dried basil, crumbled
1 teaspoon dried marjoram, crumbled
1 bay leaf
2½ pounds ground veal
1½ cups fresh bread crumbs
½ cup milk
2 eggs, beaten
2 teaspoons salt
1½ teaspoons freshly ground black pepper
Tuna Mayonnaise (recipe follows)
3 tablespoons small (nonpareil) capers, drained

1. In a large skillet, warm the olive oil over medium heat. Add the onions, garlic, basil, marjoram and bay leaf, cover and cook, stirring once or twice, until lightly colored, 8 to 10 minutes. Remove from the heat, discard the bay leaf and cool to room temperature.

2. Position a rack in the middle of the oven and preheat the oven to 350 degrees F. In a large mixing bowl, combine the ground veal, the onion mixture, bread crumbs, milk, eggs, salt and pepper and mix thoroughly. Transfer the meat mixture to a shallow baking dish and form it into a flat loaf about 2½ inches thick; smooth the top of the loaf with the back of a spoon.

3. Bake for about 1¼ hours, or until an instant-reading thermometer inserted into the center of the loaf registers 145 degrees F. Let the loaf stand on a rack until cool. *The meat loaf can be prepared 1 day ahead. Wrap well and refrigerate, returning the meat loaf to room temperature before serving.*

4. Cut the meat loaf into thin slices. Arrange the slices, slightly overlapping, on serving plates. Coat generously with Tuna Mayonnaise, sprinkle with the capers and serve cool.

Tuna Mayonnaise

Makes about 2¼ cups

This is also delicious as a dip for raw vegetables or as a sauce for poached or grilled shrimp, chicken or fish.

1 can (3¼ ounces) oil-packed tuna, drained
2 large eggs
3 oil-packed anchovy fillets
2 to 3 tablespoons fresh lemon juice
1 tablespoon small (nonpareil) capers, drained
1 teaspoon freshly ground black pepper
½ teaspoon salt
1 cup olive oil
½ cup corn oil

1. In a food processor, combine the tuna, eggs, anchovy fillets, 2 tablespoons of the lemon juice, the capers, pepper and salt. Process until smooth.

2. With the machine on, add the olive and corn oils through the feed tube in a quick, steady stream. The mayonnaise will thicken. Adjust the seasoning, adding more lemon juice and salt to taste. *The mayonnaise can be prepared up to 2 days ahead. Transfer to a storage container, cover and refrigerate.*

Basil Rice Salad with Peas and Pine Nuts

Serves 8 to 10

Cool and light, this colorful salad is the perfect accompaniment to the cold veal loaf. If you have no fresh basil, flat-leaf parsley can be substituted.

½ cup pine nuts
2½ cups water
1¼ cups long-grain rice
1½ teaspoons salt
½ cup olive oil
3 tablespoons fresh lemon juice
1 teaspoon freshly ground black pepper
1 package (10 ounces) frozen peas, thawed and drained
½ cup minced fresh basil
⅓ cup grated Parmesan cheese

1. Position a rack in the middle of the oven and preheat the oven to 375 degrees F. Spread the pine nuts in a metal baking pan and toast them, stirring once or twice, until lightly browned, 10 to 12 minutes. Remove from the pan and cool.

2. In a medium saucepan, bring the water to a boil over high heat. Stir in the rice and salt. When the water returns to a boil, turn the heat to low and cover the pan.

(continued)

Cook undisturbed for 22 minutes, or until the rice is tender and has absorbed all of the water. Let stand, covered, off the heat for 5 minutes. Transfer the rice to a large bowl and cool to room temperature, fluffing it occasionally with a fork and breaking up any clumps.

3. Stir the olive oil, lemon juice and pepper into the rice. Add the peas, basil, toasted pine nuts and Parmesan cheese and toss well. *The salad can be prepared several hours ahead. Cover and hold at room temperature.*

■ ■ ■

Finishing touches: Serve the veal loaf and rice salad with sliced tomatoes, drizzling them with some of the tuna mayonnaise. Accompany the meal with focaccia or other good bread and drink a crisp, not too dry Italian white wine (like Soave). For dessert, offer fresh strawberries with lightly sweetened ricotta or mascarpone cheese and purchased biscotti.

Leftovers: Thin slices of the cold veal loaf and any leftover tomatoes and tuna mayonnaise can be combined on crusty bread to make a wonderful sandwich (add some crisp lettuce if desired). Or the veal loaf can be diced and added to any rice to create a main-course salad.

Beef, Sausage and Spinach Loaf with Tomato-Olive Sauce

Serves 8 to 10

This flavorful loaf will remind you of good meat balls—moist and savory, fragrant and garlicky, napped with a spicy, olive-studded tomato sauce. It hardly needs saying that Italian food is always a crowd-pleaser, and this dish is no exception.

⅓ cup olive oil
2 cups finely chopped onions
4 garlic cloves, minced
1 teaspoon dried basil, crumbled
1 teaspoon dried oregano, crumbled
1 teaspoon dried thyme, crumbled
1 teaspoon crushed hot red pepper
2 packages (10 ounces each) chopped frozen spinach,
    thawed and squeezed dry
2 pounds lean ground beef
1 pound Italian-style sweet sausage, removed from its
    casing and crumbled
¾ cup fine, dry bread crumbs
3 eggs, beaten
⅓ cup grated Parmesan cheese
1 teaspoon salt
Tomato-Olive Sauce (recipe follows)

1. In a large nonreactive skillet, warm the olive oil over medium heat. Add the onions, garlic, basil, oregano, thyme and hot pepper, cover and cook, stirring once or twice, for 10 minutes. Uncover, stir in the spinach and cook, stirring to break up the clumps, for 3 minutes. Remove from the heat and cool to room temperature.

2. Position a rack in the middle of the oven and preheat the oven to 350 degrees F. In a large bowl, combine the ground beef, sausage, the spinach mixture, bread crumbs, eggs, Parmesan cheese and salt and mix thoroughly. In a shallow baking dish form the meat into a flat loaf about 2½ inches thick; smooth the top with the back of a spoon.

3. Bake the meat loaf for about 1½ hours, or until an instant-reading thermometer inserted into the center of the loaf registers 160 degrees F. Let the meat loaf rest on a rack for 10 minutes before slicing. Serve, passing the Tomato-Olive Sauce on the side.

Tomato-Olive Sauce

Makes about 3 cups

Brine-cured imported Calamata olives add a pungent note and strong color accent to this spicy tomato sauce. If you can't locate the olives (try a good cheese shop), don't substitute bland California "ripe" olives; just omit them altogether.

3 tablespoons olive oil
1 cup finely chopped onion
3 garlic cloves, minced
¾ teaspoon crushed hot red pepper
½ teaspoon dried basil, crumbled
½ teaspoon dried oregano, crumbled
½ teaspoon dried thyme leaves, crumbled
1 can (35 ounces) Italian-style plum tomatoes, with their juices
½ teaspoon salt
16 brine-cured Calamata olives, pitted and chopped
⅓ cup finely chopped flat-leaf parsley

1. In a medium, nonreactive saucepan, warm the olive oil over low heat. Add the onion, garlic, hot pepper, basil, oregano and thyme. Cover and cook, stirring once or twice, for 15 minutes. Add the tomatoes, breaking them up with a spoon, their juices and the salt. Bring to a simmer and cook uncovered, stirring occasionally, until the sauce is reduced to 3 cups, about 45 minutes.

2. Cool the sauce slightly and then force it through the medium disk of a food mill or puree until smooth in a food processor. *The sauce can be prepared to this point up to 3 days ahead. Cover and refrigerate.*

3. Reheat the sauce until simmering. Stir in the olives and parsley and season with additional salt and pepper to taste before serving.

Pesto Mashed Potatoes

Serves 8

If salsa is the ketchup of our times, surely pesto is the butter; hence this pairing of Italian basil sauce with mashed American spuds. Francine the Caterer (a purist in Mediterranean matters) views this whole idea with disapproval, but everyone for whom I've prepared it has virtually swooned. Use store-bought, refrigerated pesto for convenience or home-made pesto for superior flavor.

4½ pounds russet baking potatoes (8 to 9 large),
    peeled and chunked
1½ cups milk
1 teaspoon salt
⅔ cup prepared pesto sauce
Freshly ground black pepper
Unsalted butter, as accompaniment (optional)

1. In a large saucepan, cover the potatoes with cold salted water and set over medium heat. Bring to a boil, then lower the heat and cook uncovered, stirring once or twice, until the potatoes are very tender, about 25 minutes.

2. Meanwhile, in a small saucepan, combine the milk and salt and bring just to a simmer over low heat. Drain the potatoes and force them through the medium disk of a food mill or mash them by hand; do not use a food processor. Return the potatoes to their saucepan and set over low heat. Stir the potatoes constantly for 3 minutes. Slowly whisk in the warm milk, then stir in the pesto. Beat the potatoes for a minute or two, until they are fluffy. Add pepper generously to taste, adjust the seasoning and serve hot, passing butter at the table if desired.

■ ■ ■

Finishing touches: Serve the meat loaf with a plain green vegetable, like sautéed zucchini, or with a salad of romaine lettuce and accompany the meal with hot garlic bread. As an alternative to the mashed potatoes, you may wish to consider tossing the tomato sauce with cooked short pasta, such as penne. Drink a robust red wine, like Chianti or zinfandel. Serve ripe juicy pears and provolone cheese for dessert.

Leftovers: Arrange thin slices of meat loaf and mozzarella cheese on a hard roll. Wrap in foil and heat in the oven until the cheese melts. Serve with a dollop of left-over tomato sauce.

Eastern Mediterranean Lamb and Bulgur Loaf with Yogurt Sauce

Serves 8 to 10

This loaf takes its inspiration from the Middle Eastern dish *kibbeh*, which combines raw lamb and bulgur, a parboiled, quick-cooking cracked wheat. Baking these two ingredients into a meat loaf instead of enjoying them raw, however, transforms them into something completely American, and though it is eaten cold, with a tangy yogurt and lemon sauce, this meat loaf is nevertheless 100 percent familiar and delicious. (It's good hot, too, by the way, with the Tomato-Olive Sauce on page 46 replacing the yogurt sauce.)

1 cup canned crushed tomatoes
⅓ cup medium-grain bulgur
¼ cup olive oil
2 cups finely chopped onions
6 garlic cloves, minced
2½ pounds lean ground lamb
2 eggs, beaten
2½ teaspoons salt
1½ teaspoons freshly ground black pepper
1 container (16 ounces) plain yogurt
3 tablespoons fresh lemon juice

1. In a small bowl, combine the tomatoes and bulgur and let stand, stirring once or twice, for 30 minutes.

2. Meanwhile, in a large skillet, warm the olive oil over medium heat. Add the onions and garlic, cover and cook, stirring once or twice, for 10 minutes. Remove from the heat and cool to room temperature.

3. Position a rack in the middle of the oven and preheat the oven to 350 degrees F. In a large bowl, combine the ground lamb, the tomato-bulgur mixture, the onion mixture, eggs, 2 teaspoons of the salt and the pepper and mix thoroughly. Transfer the meat mixture to a shallow baking dish and shape it into a flat loaf about 2½ inches thick; smooth the top with the back of a spoon.

4. Bake for about 1 hour and 10 minutes, or until an instant-reading thermometer inserted into the center of the loaf registers 145 degrees F. Let the meat loaf rest on a rack until cool. The meat loaf can be prepared 1 day ahead. *Cover and refrigerate, returning the meat loaf to room temperature before serving.*

5. In a small bowl, whisk together the yogurt, lemon juice and remaining ½ teaspoon salt. Slice the meat loaf and serve, spooning some of the yogurt sauce over each slice.

White Bean, Cucumber and Tomato Salad with Feta and Fresh Mint

Serves 8 to 10

This easy salad combines both starch and vegetable in one colorful, Mediterranean-accented mélange. Basil can be substituted for the mint; goat cheese can replace the feta.

1 pound dry white kidney beans (cannellini), picked over
3 teaspoons salt
½ cup white wine vinegar
½ cup olive oil
2 medium cucumbers (about 1 pound total), peeled, seeded and cut into ½-inch chunks
1 teaspoon freshly ground black pepper
½ cup finely chopped fresh mint
⅓ cup finely chopped flat-leaf parsley
¼ pound feta cheese, drained and crumbled
2 medium ripe tomatoes (about 1 pound), trimmed and cut into thin wedges

1. In a large bowl, combine the beans with enough cold water to cover them by at least 3 inches and let stand overnight. Drain the beans. In a large pot, combine the beans with enough cold water to cover them by at least 3 inches and set over medium heat. Bring to a boil, then lower the heat and simmer, partially covered, for 20 minutes. Stir in 2 teaspoons of the salt and simmer another 15 to 20 minutes, or until the beans are just tender.

Drain immediately and transfer to a large bowl. Pour the vinegar over the hot beans and toss gently. Let the beans stand, stirring them once or twice, until cool. Stir in the olive oil. *The salad can be prepared to this point 1 day ahead. Cover and refrigerate, returning it to room temperature before proceeding.*

2. Stir in the cucumbers, the remaining 1 teaspoon salt, the pepper, mint and parsley. Fold in the feta and adjust the seasoning. Transfer the salad to a bowl or platter, and arrange the tomato wedges over the beans just before serving.

■ ■ ■

Finishing touches: Accompany the meat loaf and beans with warmed pita breads and drink a chilled fruity white wine. For dessert, offer slices of fresh melon drizzled with honey and plain butter cookies.

Leftovers: Cut leftover meat loaf into ¾-inch cubes. Toss them with leftover bean salad, add more oil and vinegar if necessary and serve in warmed pitas or atop a bed of salad greens.

Sherried Teriyaki Turkey Loaf

Serves 6 to 8

This doesn't have very much to do with the Japanese grilled dish from which it takes its name, but the ready availability of bottled teriyaki marinades and glazes compelled me to fashion a meat loaf taking advantage of them. Fresh ginger, a touch of sherry and a dollop of orange marmalade add welcome depth of flavor, and the resulting sweet-salty taste complements turkey nicely.

½ stick (4 tablespoons) unsalted butter
2 cups finely chopped onions
1 tablespoon grated fresh ginger
2 garlic cloves, minced
⅓ cup plus 1 tablespoon medium-dry sherry
2 pounds ground turkey
2 eggs, beaten
½ cup rolled oats
1½ teaspoons salt
¾ teaspoon freshly ground black pepper
½ cup thick teriyaki baste and glaze
½ cup orange marmalade

1. In a large skillet, melt the butter over medium heat. When it foams, add the onions, ginger and garlic, cover and cook, stirring once or twice, until the onion is lightly colored, 8 to 10 minutes. Add ⅓ cup of the sherry, raise the heat to medium-high and boil, stirring often, until the sherry is reduced to a glaze that just coats the onions, about 2 minutes. Cool to room temperature.

2. Position a rack in the middle of the oven and preheat the oven to 350 degrees F. In a large bowl, combine the ground turkey, the onion mixture, eggs, oats, salt and pepper and mix thoroughly. Transfer the meat mixture to a shallow baking dish and shape it into a flat loaf about 2½ inches thick; smooth the top with the back of a spoon. In a small bowl, stir together the teriyaki baste, orange marmalade and remaining 1 tablespoon sherry.

3. Baste the loaf with half of the teriyaki mixture. Bake the loaf for 25 minutes. Baste with half the remaining teriyaki mixture and bake the loaf for 15 minutes. Baste the loaf with the remaining teriyaki mixture and bake for another 15 minutes, or until an instant-reading thermometer inserted into the center of the loaf registers 160 degrees F. Let the loaf rest at least 10 minutes before slicing. Serve hot.

Gingered Baby Carrots

Serves 6 to 8

Fresh baby carrots, peeled, bagged and ready to cook, are increasingly found in produce stores and some supermarkets, while the frozen version is more widely available. Either way, they're sweet, tender and rather cute, sort of an automatic garnish as well as a side dish, and the convenience of not peeling the little devils can't be denied. If you don't find them, substitute regular carrots, peeled and cut crosswise into 1½-inch sections. These won't be as cute, but will certainly be as delicious, thanks to the sweet gingery glaze.

2 pounds fresh or thawed baby carrots, peeled and trimmed
2 teaspoons salt
½ stick (4 tablespoons) unsalted butter
2 teaspoons grated fresh ginger
2 garlic cloves, minced
1 cup chicken stock or canned broth
2 teaspoons soy sauce
2 teaspoons sugar
½ teaspoon freshly ground black pepper

1. Bring a large pot of water to a boil. Add the carrots and salt and cook, stirring once or twice, until the carrots are just tender, about 4 minutes after the water returns to the boil. Drain into a colander and rinse under cold running water; drain well. *The carrots can be prepared to this point up to one day ahead. Wrap well and refrigerate.*

2. In a large skillet, melt the butter over low heat. When it foams, add the ginger and garlic, cover and cook, stirring once or twice, for 5 minutes. Add the carrots, stock, soy sauce and sugar. Raise the heat and bring to a brisk simmer. Cook, stirring and tossing the carrots in the stock, for about 10 minutes, or until it has reduced to a glaze that just coats them. Stir in the pepper. Serve hot.

■ ■ ■

Finishing touches: Serve the turkey loaf and glazed carrots with steamed white rice, if you wish, or offer buttered mashed potatoes. Beer goes well with the slightly salty teriyaki glaze, and a Japanese beer like Sapporo would be a fine choice. For dessert, serve chilled fresh seasonal fruit.

Leftovers: Serve the turkey loaf cold, accompanied by a green salad dressed with a teriyaki vinaigrette.

Swedish Meat Loaf with Creamy Dilled Pan Gravy

Serves 6 to 8

I don't know if Swedish meat balls are actually Swedish, but I do know the tender, nutmeg-spiced, veal-based morsels, often swimming in a creamy dill sauce, are an utterly delicious way to use ground meat—hence this recipe.

½ stick (4 tablespoons) unsalted butter
2 cups finely chopped onions
1 pound ground veal
1 pound ground pork
1 cup soft, fresh bread crumbs
½ cup milk
2 eggs, beaten
2½ teaspoons salt
1½ teaspoons freshly ground black pepper
⅜ teaspoon freshly grated nutmeg
⅛ teaspoon ground allspice
2 tablespoons unbleached all-purpose flour
1 cup chicken stock or canned broth
1 cup whipping cream or heavy cream
¼ cup minced fresh dill
1 tablespoon Dijon-style mustard

1. In a large skillet, melt the butter over medium heat. When it foams, add the onions, cover and cook, stirring once or twice, for 10 minutes. Remove from the heat and cool to room temperature.

2. In a large bowl, combine the ground veal and pork, the onion mixture, bread crumbs, milk, eggs, 2 teaspoons of the salt, 1 teaspoon of the pepper, ¼ teaspoon of the nutmeg and the allspice and mix thoroughly. Transfer the meat mixture to a shallow flameproof baking dish and shape it into a flat loaf about 2½ inches thick; smooth the top with the back of a spoon.

3. Bake the meat loaf for about 1¼ hours, or until an instant-reading thermometer inserted into the center registers 160 degrees F. Let rest for 5 minutes. Transfer the loaf to a serving platter and keep warm.

4. Pour off all but 2 tablespoons of drippings from the baking dish and set it over low heat. Whisk in the flour and cook, stirring often, for 3 minutes. Whisk in the stock, cream, and the remaining ½ teaspoon each salt and pepper and ⅛ teaspoon nutmeg. Raise the heat slightly and bring the gravy to a simmer. Cook, stirring often and scraping the sides and bottom of the dish, until the gravy thickens slightly, about 4 minutes. Whisk in the dill and mustard.

5. Slice the meat loaf and serve it hot, napped with the gravy.

Rutabaga, Carrot and Shallot Pudding

Serves 6 to 8

The rutabaga is also called a swede turnip, which possibly means this smooth and creamy root vegetable side dish has more claim to authenticity than the preceding meat loaf. This recipe illustrates one of my favorite food theories (from the poet Paul Hecht) that things of a similar color taste good together. The sweetness of the carrots mellows the rutabagas' odd bitterness, and taken together the vegetables are far more delicious than the sum of their humble parts.

2 medium rutabagas (about 1½ pounds total),
    trimmed, peeled and cut into ½-inch chunks
8 large carrots (about 1½ pounds), trimmed, peeled
    and cut into ½-inch chunks
3 cups chicken stock or canned broth
8 large shallots, peeled
1 stick (8 tablespoons) unsalted butter
⅓ cup sugar
¼ teaspoon freshly grated nutmeg
1 cup whipping cream or heavy cream
6 eggs
1½ teaspoons salt
1 teaspoon freshly ground black pepper

1. In a large saucepan, combine the rutabagas, carrots, chicken stock, shallots, butter, sugar and nutmeg. Bring to a boil over medium heat, then lower the heat slightly and cook, stirring occasionally, until the vegetables are very tender, about 40 minutes.

2. With a slotted spoon transfer the vegetables to a food processor. Set the pot over high heat and bring to a boil. Cook hard, stirring constantly, for about 5 minutes, or until the liquid is reduced to ¼ cup. Add the liquid to the food processor and puree until very smooth. Add the cream and process again to blend. Cool to room temperature. *The recipe can be prepared to this point up to 1 day ahead. Cover and refrigerate, returning the puree to room temperature before proceeding.*

3. Position a rack in the middle of the oven and preheat the oven to 350 degrees F. Butter a 3-quart baking or soufflé dish about 6 inches deep. Whisk the eggs into the vegetable puree. Whisk in the salt and pepper. Pour the mixture into the prepared dish.

4. Bake the pudding for about 50 minutes, until puffed, firm and golden. Let the pudding rest on a rack for 5 minutes before serving.

■ ■ ■

Finishing touches: Serve the meat loaf and pudding with Lemon-Parsley New Potatoes (page 119) or with buttered mashed potatoes. Black bread and a crisp, herbaceous wine, such as Gewürztraminer or Riesling, would be fine accompaniments. For dessert, serve fresh strawberries or blueberries, sauced with pureed raspberries and garnished with whipped cream.

Leftovers: Oven warm foil-wrapped slices of the meat loaf, moistened with a bit of the gravy and serve on sandwiches of black bread.

Chutney-Glazed Curried Beef Loaf

Serves 8 to 10

Curry blends, like chili powders, vary widely, and a serious cook (or at least a curry-loving one) will have a preferred brand or two or three, using one or the other according to the dish being prepared. My favorite label is Lawrence, mail-ordered from an obscure New England company, but Sun brand, which is widely available, is a good alternative, and even supermarket powders can be used in the following, an intensely curry-flavored meat loaf topped with sweet and spicy mango chutney.

5 tablespoons unsalted butter
2 cups finely chopped onions
4 garlic cloves, minced
3 tablespoons mild but flavorful curry powder
½ teaspoon crushed hot red pepper
¼ teaspoon ground cinnamon
¼ teaspoon ground ginger
1 can (8 ounces) tomato sauce
2½ pounds ground beef
2 eggs, beaten
1 cup fine, dry bread crumbs
2½ teaspoons salt
1 teaspoon freshly ground black pepper
1 jar (about 8 ounces) mango chutney

1. In a large nonreactive skillet, melt the butter over medium heat. When it foams, add the onions and garlic, cover and cook, stirring once or twice, for 5 minutes. Add the curry powder, crushed hot pepper, cinnamon and ginger and cook, covered, stirring often, for 5 minutes. Add the tomato sauce and bring to a simmer. Cook uncovered, stirring once or twice, for 5 minutes. Remove from the heat and cool to room temperature.

2. Position a rack in the middle of the oven and preheat the oven to 350 degrees F. In a large bowl, combine the ground beef, the curried tomato-onion mixture, eggs, bread crumbs, salt and pepper and mix thoroughly. Transfer the meat mixture to a shallow baking dish and shape it into a flat loaf about 2½ inches thick; smooth the top of the loaf with the back of a spoon. Spread the chutney evenly atop the loaf.

3. Bake for about 1 hour and 20 minutes, or until an instant-reading thermometer inserted into the center registers 145 degrees F. Let the meat loaf rest on a rack for 10 minutes before slicing. Serve hot.

Spicy Lentils with Peas and Tomatoes

Serves 8 to 10

This colorful side dish goes together easily and quickly, providing both the starch and vegetable accompaniment to the curried beef loaf. Fresh mint can replace part or all of the cilantro.

1 pound dried lentils, picked over and rinsed
3 teaspoons salt
5 tablespoons unsalted butter
1 fresh jalapeño chile, minced
2 garlic cloves, minced
1 pound fresh plum tomatoes (about 6 medium), cut into ¾-inch chunks
1 package (10 ounces) frozen peas, defrosted and well drained
⅓ cup minced fresh cilantro

1. Bring a large saucepan of water to a boil. Add the lentils and 2 teaspoons of the salt and simmer, stirring once or twice, until the lentils are just tender, about 20 minutes. Drain. *The lentils can be prepared up to 1 day ahead. Cover and refrigerate.*

2. In a large nonreactive skillet, melt the butter over low heat. When it foams, stir in the jalapeño and garlic, cover and cook, stirring once or twice, for 5 minutes. Add the tomatoes and cook uncovered, stirring once or twice, for 2 minutes. Add the lentils, peas and remaining 1 tea-spoon salt and cook, covered, stirring once or twice, for 5 minutes, or until heated through and steaming. Stir in the cilantro and adjust the seasoning. Serve hot.

■ ■ ■

Finishing touches: Serve the meal with warmed flour tortillas or pita breads, which will have to stand in for such authentic Indian breads as pooris and chapatis. Drink fresh lemonade, limeade or a well-chilled beer, and for dessert, offer either rice pudding, well spiced with cinnamon, or a purchased fruit sorbet and plain sugar cookies.

Leftovers: Slice leftover meat loaf thinly, arrange it over a salad of greens and sliced apples and dress it with a curry-spiked vinaigrette.

██

Chapter Three

UPWARDLY MOBILE MEAT LOAVES

Recipes for the Modern Gourmet

It was bound to happen. Our craving for comfort has caused us to hunger for meat loaf, and in reaching into the well-stocked cupboard (Stardate: Supper Time, 1993) for the bread crumbs, ketchup and garlic powder, we have accidentally grabbed instead the balsamic vinegar, hot pepper jelly and dried porcini mushrooms. As good cooks will do, especially good modern cooks, we have not let the rumbling in our stomachs drown out that little voice of inspiration whispering in our ear, "Oh, come on, give it a try." With a sudden lurch the meat loaf has been dragged into the modern age, and like other easy-going food favorites (chocolate chip cookies, tamales, chili, mashed potatoes), it has accommodated to our impetuous improvisations with ease, seemingly transformed into something excitingly fresh and new to eat, while remaining satisfyingly old-fashioned at heart. Don't let the roasted garlic, goat cheese and fresh herbs fool you—the following upwardly mobile loaves are as comfortable and familiar as the hungriest old-timer could want.

██

57

Double Mushroom Pork and Veal Loaf with Fresh Thyme

Serves 6 to 8

Two kinds of mushrooms plus pork and veal combine in a rich, subtle meat loaf that is as hearty and reassuring as comfort cooking should be. Use leftover Chinese carry-out rice or simmer ¼ cup long-grain rice in 1½ cups water until almost tender, about 15 minutes, and then drain it in a sieve.

1½ cups chicken stock or canned broth
1 ounce dried porcini or cèpe mushrooms (about 1 cup), rinsed
½ pound fresh white mushrooms, trimmed
¾ stick (6 tablespoons) unsalted butter
2 cups finely chopped onions
½ cup whipping cream or heavy cream
⅔ cup cooked white rice
3 tablespoons fresh thyme leaves or 2 teaspoons dried, crumbled
2 garlic cloves, minced
2 teaspoons salt
1 teaspoon freshly ground black pepper
1½ pounds ground pork
1 pound ground veal
2 eggs, beaten

1. In a small saucepan, bring the chicken stock to a boil. In a small heatproof bowl, combine the hot stock and the dried mushrooms. Cover and let stand until cool, about 30 minutes.

2. With a slotted spoon, transfer the softened mushrooms to a food processor. Let the mushroom soaking liquid settle, then pour off and reserve the clear portion, discarding the gritty residue. Add the fresh mushrooms to the soaked mushrooms in the food processor and finely chop them.

3. In a large skillet, melt the butter over medium-high heat. When it foams, add the onions and chopped mushrooms and cook uncovered, stirring often, until lightly browned, about 8 minutes. Stir in the mushroom soaking liquid, cream, rice, thyme and garlic and cook uncovered, stirring frequently, until the mixture is reduced and very thick, about 5 minutes. Remove from the heat, stir in the salt and pepper and cool to room temperature.

4. Position a rack in the middle of the oven and preheat the oven to 350 degrees F. In a large bowl, combine the ground pork and veal, the mushroom mixture and eggs and mix thoroughly. Transfer the meat mixture to a shallow baking dish and form into a flat loaf about 2½ inches thick; smooth the top with the back of a spoon.

5. Bake for about 1 hour and 20 minutes, or until an instant-reading thermometer inserted into the center of the loaf registers 160 degrees F. Let the meat loaf rest on a rack for 10 minutes before slicing. Serve hot.

Potato and Celery Root Gratin

Serves 6 to 8

In season from late fall to early spring, celery root, or celeriac, is a type of celery cultivated for its bulbous root, which is about the most celery-intensive thing you're ever likely to run across. The root combines well with neutral potatoes in this slow-baked, crusty gratin. If you have no celeriac, just increase the potatoes to 3½ pounds for a fine potato gratin.

1½ pounds celery root (about 2 medium)
2¾ teaspoons salt
2 pounds russet baking potatoes (3 or 4 large)
¾ teaspoon freshly ground black pepper
1½ cups chicken stock or canned broth
½ cup crème fraîche, whipping cream or heavy cream
2 tablespoons butter, cut in small pieces

1. Peel the celery root with a paring knife. Halve each and cut each half into ¼-inch-thick slices. Bring a medium saucepan of water to a boil. Stir in 2 teaspoons of the salt, add the celery root and cook (though the water need not return to the boil) for 3 minutes. Drain and transfer immediately to a large bowl of ice water. Cool completely and drain thoroughly.

2. Position a rack in the middle of the oven and preheat the oven to 350 degrees F. Butter a shallow 6-cup baking dish. Arrange the celery root and potatoes in layers in the prepared dish, ending with a potato layer. Lightly season the layers with the salt and pepper as you work. In a small bowl, stir together the stock and crème fraîche. Pour the stock mixture evenly over the layered vegetables and dot the top with the butter.

3. Bake for about 1½ hours, or until the top of the gratin is browned and the vegetables have absorbed most of the liquid. Let the gratin rest on a rack for 10 minutes before serving. Serve hot.

■ ■ ■

Finishing touches: Serve the meat loaf and gratin with broiled, bread crumb-topped tomatoes or another colorful vegetable. Accompany the meal with crusty bread and sweet butter and drink a light, simple red wine, such as a grand cru Beaujolais or a pinot noir from Oregon or Washington. For dessert, offer apples or pears, poached in white wine, accompanied by nut cookies.

Leftovers: This loaf makes a fine sandwich, served on whole grain bread with thin slices of unpeeled pears, Swiss cheese and horseradish mayonnaise.

Two-Meat Meat Loaf with Sun-Dried Tomatoes

Serves 6 to 8

In the modern kitchen, where sun-dried tomatoes are as common as ketchup, this meat loaf qualifies as home cookin'. The recipe, adapted from my book, *The New American Kitchen*, has turned out to be one of the most popular dishes from that collection of menus for casual entertaining. Friends in Texas prepare it often, friends in California make it to sell in their wine country grocery store, and with all the meat loaf recipes at my disposal, it's the one I cook most often at home.

¼ cup olive oil
1½ cups finely chopped onions
½ cup finely chopped celery
3 garlic cloves, minced
1 teaspoon dried basil, crumbled
1 teaspoon dried oregano, crumbled
1 teaspoon dried thyme leaves, crumbled
1½ pounds ground beef
1 pound Italian-style sweet sausage, casings removed
½ cup coarsely chopped oil-packed sun-dried
   tomatoes

½ cup finely chopped flat-leaf parsley
2 eggs, beaten
½ cup fine, dry bread crumbs
1½ teaspoons salt
1½ teaspoons freshly ground black pepper

1. In a large skillet, warm the olive oil over medium heat. Add the onions, celery, garlic, basil, oregano and thyme, cover and cook, stirring once or twice, for 10 minutes. Remove from the heat and cool to room temperature.

2. Position a rack in the middle of the oven and preheat the oven to 350 degrees F. In a large bowl, mix together the ground beef, sausage, the onion mixture, sun-dried tomatoes, parsley, eggs, bread crumbs, salt and pepper. Transfer the meat mixture to a shallow baking dish and shape it into a flat loaf about 2½ inches thick; smooth the top of the loaf with the back of a spoon.

3. Bake about 1½ hours, or until an instant-reading thermometer inserted into the center of the loaf registers 165 degrees F. Let rest on a rack for 10 minutes before slicing. Serve hot.

Peppery Pan-Grilled Polenta

Serves 6 to 8

Polenta is Italian cornmeal mush. It can be served in hot, creamy mounds, just like mashed potatoes (don't forget the butter), or it can be poured into a pan, chilled, cut into pieces and then grilled or sautéed. Crisp on the outside, hot and grainy within, such twice-cooked polenta is not only delicious, but convenient, since the lengthy simmering and stirring stage is gotten out of the way well in advance. The polenta can be cooked over an open flame, if desired, or (less bother) pan-fried on a ridged, cast-iron stovetop grilling pan. Top the polenta, if you like, with curls of genuine Parmigiano Reggiano or crumbled Gorgonzola dolcelatte cheese.

About ⅓ cup olive oil
1 cup yellow cornmeal, preferably stone ground
4 cups water
1½ teaspoons salt
1½ teaspoons freshly ground black pepper

1. Lightly brush an 8-inch square baking pan with some of the olive oil. Measure the cornmeal into a large heavy saucepan. Slowly whisk in the water. Set the pan over medium heat and stir in the salt and pepper. Bring to a simmer, stirring often. Reduce the heat to medium-low, partially cover the pan (the polenta will spatter as it thickens) and cook, stirring often, for 25 minutes. Remove from the heat and pour the polenta into the pre-

pared pan. Cool to room temperature, cover and refrigerate until cold and firm, at least 5 hours. *The polenta can be prepared up to 2 days ahead.*

2. Invert the pan onto a work surface; the chilled polenta will drop out. With a long, sharp knife cut the polenta into 12 equal rectangular pieces. Set a ridged stovetop grill pan or a cast-iron skillet over medium-high heat. Brush it generously with some of the oil. When it is very hot, grill a few of the polenta pieces, turning once or twice, until they are lightly browned by the grill pan and are heated through. Transfer them to a heated platter; repeat with the remaining polenta, wiping the grill pan free of blackened bits and re-oiling it between batches. Serve the polenta hot or warm.

■ ■ ■

Finishing touches: Serve the meat loaf and polenta with a simple sautéed green vegetable, such as zucchini, sprinkled after cooking with a little grated Parmesan cheese. Serve crusty bread and drink a robust red wine like zinfandel. For dessert, serve ice cream, drizzled with Galliano or Strega liqueur, accompanied by espresso.

Leftovers: This meat loaf makes a great sandwich. Serve it on small hard rolls, accompanied by a generous dollop of lemony garlic mayonnaise.

Smoked Three-Meat Loaf

Serves 6 to 8

Smoke adds a subtle but important flavor element to this otherwise simple meat loaf. Widely available and very affordable, home water smokers (Brinkman and Rival are two popular brands) can be used to cook almost any meat loaf. The basic ingredients are compatible with the taste of hickory, mesquite and other savory smoking woods. The meat loaf is sliced and then served atop a mound of Sweet and Sour Red Cabbage (recipe follows).

3 or 4 chunks of smoking wood, preferably hickory or fruitwood
½ stick (4 tablespoons) unsalted butter
1½ cups finely chopped onions
½ cup finely chopped celery
1 pound ground beef
½ pound ground pork
½ pound ground veal
2 eggs, beaten
½ cup corn flake crumbs
⅓ cup milk
2 tablespoons prepared horseradish, preferably red
2 teaspoons salt
1 teaspoon freshly ground black pepper
½ cup honey mustard

1. Soak the wood chunks in water for at least 2 hours. Set up a water smoker outdoors in a place shielded from the wind.

2. In a large skillet, melt the butter over medium heat. When it foams, add the onions and celery and cook covered, stirring once or twice, until the vegetables are tender and lightly colored, 8 to 10 minutes. Remove from the heat and cool to room temperature.

3. In a large bowl, combine the ground beef, pork and veal with the onion mixture, eggs, corn flake crumbs, milk, horseradish, salt and pepper and mix thoroughly. In a shallow, disposable foil pan just large enough to set on a rack of the smoker you are using, shape the meat into a rectangular loaf about 4 inches thick. Spread the honey mustard evenly over the top of the loaf.

4. Drain the wood chunks. Place them in the smoker and set the basin of water in place according to the manufacturer's directions. Set the meat loaf on the upper rack, cover the smoker and smoke the meat loaf for 1½ to 2 hours, depending on wind, weather and the smoker you use. When the meat loaf is done, an instant-reading thermometer inserted into the center of the loaf will register 160 degrees F. Let rest for 10 minutes before slicing. Serve the meat loaf atop the sweet and sour cabbage.

Sweet and Sour Red Cabbage

Serves 6 to 8

This quick sauté of cabbage and apples gets its sour and most of its sweet from rich, dark Italian balsamic wine vinegar. Produced in and around the Modena area, it is one of Italy's finest exports.

5 tablespoons unsalted butter
2 large leeks (white part only), well cleaned and finely chopped
2 medium tart apples, such as Granny Smith, cored, peeled and coarsely chopped
9 cups coarsely shredded red cabbage (from a 1½- to 2-pound cabbage)
⅓ cup balsamic vinegar
⅓ cup chicken stock or canned broth
1 tablespoon sugar
¾ teaspoon salt
½ teaspoon freshly ground black pepper

1. In a large, nonreactive flameproof casserole, melt the butter over medium heat. When it foams, stir in the leeks and apples, cover and cook, stirring once or twice, until very tender, 8 to 10 minutes.

2. Stir in the red cabbage, cover and cook, stirring and tossing occasionally, until the cabbage is almost tender, about 15 minutes.

3. Uncover the skillet and stir in the vinegar, chicken stock, sugar, salt and pepper. Raise the heat slightly and cook, tossing and stirring often, for 3 minutes.

4. Divide the cabbage among the serving plates. Top the cabbage with slices of Smoked Three-Meat Loaf and serve hot.

■ ■ ■

Finishing touches: The smoky meat loaf and tangy cabbage sauté demand a rich but otherwise neutral accompaniment, such as The Mashed Potatoes (page 75) or Shiitake Mushroom Rice (page 117). Serve a coarse, whole grain bread and drink a dark, foaming beer such as Anchor Steam. For dessert, perhaps a compote of wine-simmered dried fruit and plain butter cookies.

Leftovers: Leftover smoked meat loaf is a great treat. Dice it and add to a German potato salad; use it in a sandwich of dark bread with Swiss cheese and honey mustard; or serve it cold, sliced thin, with an assortment of deli salads.

Venison Ring with Brandied Cherry Sauce

Serves 10 to 12

Venison is chief among the farm-raised game meats now available in gourmet grocery stores, a boon to the nonhunter who still wants to enjoy its deep, rich flavor. The price is high, qualifying a venison-based meat loaf like this one as an extraordinary treat. On the other hand, hunters who bag their own game and take it to a local meat locker for butchering and storage, often end up with several pounds of ground venison, and for them this will qualify as a frugal, almost inexpensive supper. Either way, it is meat loaf at its grandest, baked into a ring mold and served with a brandied cherry sauce.

3½ cups chicken stock or canned broth
½ cup brandy
2 bay leaves
1 cup tart dried cherries (about 5 ounces)
½ stick (4 tablespoons) unsalted butter
2 cups finely chopped onions
1 large leek (white part only), well cleaned and finely chopped (about 1 cup)
1 teaspoon dried thyme leaves, crumbled

2 pounds ground venison
1 pound ground pork
3 eggs, beaten
1 cup soft, fresh bread crumbs
2¾ teaspoons salt
1¾ teaspoons freshly ground black pepper
3 tablespoons cornstarch

1. In a medium saucepan, combine the chicken stock, brandy and bay leaves. Bring to a boil. In a heatproof bowl, combine the hot liquid and the cherries and cool to room temperature, stirring once or twice.

2. In a large skillet, melt the butter over medium heat. When it foams, add the onions, leek and thyme, cover and cook, stirring once or twice, until the vegetables are tender and lightly colored, 8 to 10 minutes. Cool to room temperature.

3. Position a rack in the middle of the oven and preheat the oven to 350 degrees F. In a large bowl, combine the ground venison and pork with the onion mixture, eggs, bread crumbs, 2½ teaspoons of the salt and 1½ teaspoons of the pepper and blend well. Transfer the meat mixture to a 9- or 10-cup ring pan, such as a Bundt, patting it evenly into the pan and smoothing the top flat with the back of a spoon.

4. Bake for about 1 hour and 20 minutes, or until an instant-reading thermometer inserted into the center of the loaf registers 160 degrees F. Let the loaf stand on a rack for 10 minutes.

5. Meanwhile, strain the chicken broth mixture, reserving the cherries. Measure out and separately reserve 3 tablespoons of the stock. In a medium nonreactive saucepan, bring the remaining stock and bay leaves to a boil over high heat. Boil, skimming the surface, until the stock is reduced by one-third, about 10 minutes. Turn the heat to low. In a small bowl, stir the reserved 3 tablespoons stock into the cornstarch. Slowly whisk the cornstarch mixture into the reduced stock. Stir in the cherries and the remaining ¼ teaspoon each salt and pepper. Simmer, stirring often, until the liquid thickens and becomes translucent, about 3 minutes. Remove and discard the bay leaves.

6. Pour off any unabsorbed juices remaining in the meat loaf pan. Cover the pan with a platter and invert the pan and platter together; the meat loaf will drop onto the platter. With a paper towel blot up any juices from the platter. Spoon the cherry sauce evenly over the venison loaf, filling the central well and spooning the rest around the loaf. Serve hot.

Baked Four-Grain Dressing with Mushrooms

Serves 10 to 12

Two kinds of mushrooms, four types of grain and sweet, nutty Madeira wine make this a rich and deeply flavored side dish. The less familiar among these grains are best located in a good health food store. The wheat berries must be soaked for 24 hours before cooking, so plan accordingly.

1 cup (about 6½ ounces) wheat berries, rinsed
8 cups chicken stock or canned broth
1½ ounces dried porcini (cèpe) mushrooms (about 1½ cups), rinsed
1 stick (8 tablespoons) unsalted butter
2 cups finely chopped onions
4 medium carrots, peeled and finely chopped
1 teaspoon dried thyme leaves, crumbled
2 bay leaves
1 cup dry Madeira wine, preferably Rainwater
2 teaspoons salt
1½ teaspoons freshly ground black pepper
1 cup brown rice (about 6½ ounces), preferably Wehani, rinsed
1 pound fresh white mushrooms, quartered
1 cup barley (about 6½ ounces), rinsed
1 cup quinoa (about 6½ ounces), rinsed
¾ cup finely chopped flat-leaf parsley

(continued)

1. In a medium bowl, cover the wheat berries with cold water and soak for 24 hours.

2. In a small saucepan, bring 2 cups of the chicken stock to a boil. In a small heatproof bowl, pour the hot stock over the porcini mushrooms. Let stand, stirring once or twice, until cool. With a slotted spoon, remove the mushrooms from the liquid. Chop the mushrooms. Let the liquid settle, and then pour off and reserve the clear portion, discarding the gritty residue on the bottom.

3. Position a rack in the middle of the oven and preheat the oven to 350 degrees F. In a 5-quart flameproof casserole or Dutch oven, melt 4 tablespoons of the butter over medium heat. When it foams, add the onions, carrots, minced porcini, thyme and bay leaves. Cover and cook, stirring once or twice, until the vegetables are tender and lightly colored, 8 to 10 minutes. Add the reserved mushroom soaking liquid, Madeira, remaining 6 cups chicken broth, 1½ teaspoons of the salt and 1 teaspoon of the pepper. Drain the wheat berries and stir them and the Wehani brown rice into the liquid. Bring to a simmer. Cover and bake for 35 minutes.

4. Meanwhile, in a large skillet, melt the remaining 4 tablespoons butter over medium-high heat. When it foams, add the fresh mushrooms and cook, tossing and stirring, until lightly colored, about 7 minutes. Stir in the remaining ½ teaspoon each salt and pepper and remove from the heat.

5. Stir the sautéed mushrooms, their juices, the barley and quinoa into the dressing and continue to bake, covered, until all of the liquid has been absorbed and the grains are just tender, about 30 minutes. Transfer the casserole to a rack, stir half the parsley into the dressing and let stand, covered, for 10 minutes. Spoon the dressing into a serving dish, sprinkle with the remaining parsley and serve hot.

■ ■ ■

Finishing touches: Accompany the venison ring and dressing with a plain but earthy green vegetable, like buttered brussels sprouts, or prepare Sweet and Sour Red Cabbage (page 63) or Well-Cheddared Broccoli (page 79). Serve warm corn bread and drink an excellent California or Washington State pinot noir. Dessert should be something bright and tart—cranberry cobbler, lemon mousse or a citrus sorbet.

Leftovers: The cherry sauce keeps the meat loaf moist when wrapped in foil and oven-warmed for another meal.

Veal, Roasted Red Pepper and Chèvre Loaf with Baked Garlic Gravy

Serves 6 to 8

I've packed a number of eighties' culinary clichés into one loaf on purpose, if only to prove that before they were trendy, they were good to eat and remain so. The fragrance of this savory loaf baking in the oven, and its garlicky gravy, will earn these particular clichés renewed respect.

1 large, heavy red bell pepper
¼ cup plus 3 tablespoons olive oil
2 cups finely chopped onions
¼ pound mild, fresh goat cheese (chèvre), at room temperature
1 pound ground veal
1 pound ground pork
½ cup fine, dry, seasoned bread crumbs
2 eggs, beaten
2 teaspoons salt
1½ teaspoons freshly ground black pepper
20 large unpeeled garlic cloves
3 tablespoons unbleached all-purpose flour
1¾ cups chicken stock or canned broth

1. In the open flame of a gas burner, or under a pre-heated broiler, roast the bell pepper, turning it, until the peel is evenly charred. In a closed paper bag or in a bowl covered with a plate, steam the pepper until cool. Rub away the burnt peel and stem and core the pepper. In a blender or a small food processor, puree the pepper.

2. In a large skillet, warm ¼ cup of the olive oil over medium heat. Add the onions, cover and cook, stirring once or twice, until tender and lightly colored, 8 to 10 minutes. Remove from the heat and stir in the goat cheese, mashing it into the onions until smooth. Cool to room temperature.

3. Position a rack in the middle of the oven and preheat the oven to 350 degrees F. In a large bowl, combine the ground veal and pork with the onion mixture, pepper puree, bread crumbs, eggs, salt and 1 teaspoon of the pepper and blend well. Transfer the meat mixture to a shallow baking dish, forming it into a loaf about 2½ inches high and leaving a clear space around the loaf in the bottom of the pan. Smooth the top of the loaf with the back of a spoon.

4. Bake the loaf for 30 minutes. In a small bowl, toss the garlic cloves with 1 tablespoon of the olive oil. Scatter the garlic cloves in the pan around the loaf and bake for another 50 minutes, stirring the garlic cloves from time to time. The garlic cloves should be softened within their skins and an instant-reading thermometer inserted into the center of the loaf should register 160 degrees F. Let the loaf rest on a rack for 10 minutes.

5. Meanwhile, force the garlic cloves through a food mill fitted with the fine disk or press them through a sieve with the back of a spoon; discard the skins. In a small saucepan, combine the garlic puree and the remaining 2 tablespoons olive oil over low heat. Whisk in the flour and cook, stirring often, for 3 minutes. Whisk in the chicken stock and remaining ½ teaspoon pepper; season with salt to taste. Simmer the gravy, skimming occasionally until thickened, about 4 minutes.

6. Slice the meat loaf and serve it, napped with the gravy.

Braised Fennel

Serves 6 to 8

Fennel, with its light licorice flavor, complements the garlicky meat loaf nicely, and this easy braised version cooks right in the oven along with the meat loaf. The season for fennel runs from fall through spring. Look for firm, heavy bulbs free from brown spots. For this dish to be at its best, the cheese really should be genuine imported Parmigiano Reggiano.

3 large fennel bulbs (about 3 pounds total)
1 cup beef stock or reduced-sodium canned broth
2 tablespoons unsalted butter
Salt
¼ teaspoon freshly ground black pepper
¼ cup grated Parmesan cheese

1. Position a rack in the middle of the oven and preheat the oven to 350 degrees F. Trim away the fronds and stalks of the fennel bulbs and, with a vegetable peeler, remove any tough outer skin. Slice the bulbs ½ inch thick.

2. Arrange the fennel, in a sightly overlapping layer, in a shallow casserole with a lid. Pour the stock over the fennel, dot with the butter, cover and bake for 30 minutes.

3. Uncover the casserole and bake for another 20 to 30 minutes, or until the fennel is tender and the stock has reduced to about ⅓ cup. Transfer the fennel to a serving dish. Season the stock with salt to taste and the pepper. Pour the stock over the fennel, sprinkle the grated cheese on top and serve hot.

■ ■ ■

Finishing touches: Start the meal with a salad of mixed lettuces, dressed with olive oil and sherry wine vinegar. Serve the meat loaf and braised fennel with Pesto Mashed Potatoes (page 47) or Shiitake Mushroom Rice (page 117). Offer crusty bread and pour a light, fruity red wine, such as a Chianti or Beaujolais. For dessert, serve another delicious Eighties cliché, crème brûlée.

Leftovers: Top slices of meat loaf with pieces of fennel, wrap them in foil and oven warm them, making a sandwich on a crusty sourdough baguette.

Herb Garden Buttermilk Meat Loaf

Serves 8 to 10

Fresh herbs, in astonishing variety, are now found in many fine groceries, letting good cooks celebrate their use as never before. Others, not willing to pay corsage prices for plants that often run wild, prefer to grow their own. Either way this loaf is one place to celebrate the herbal abundance. Chicken and veal keep things light, letting the flavors of the herbs shine, and buttermilk adds moisture and a touch of acidity. This loaf can be served cold, accompanied, if you wish, by the Tuna Mayonnaise on page 43.

½ stick (4 tablespoons) unsalted butter
2 cups finely chopped onions
½ cup finely chopped celery
½ cup finely chopped flat-leaf parsley
¼ cup minced assorted fresh herbs, such as sage, rosemary and thyme
1 pound ground chicken
1 pound ground veal
½ pound ground pork
⅔ cup soft, fresh bread crumbs
⅓ cup buttermilk
2 eggs, beaten
2 teaspoons salt
1½ teaspoons freshly ground black pepper

1. In a large skillet, melt the butter over medium heat. When it foams, add the onions and celery, cover and cook, stirring once or twice, until the vegetables are tender and lightly colored, 8 to 10 minutes. Remove from the heat, stir in the parsley and herbs and cool to room temperature.

2. Position a rack in the middle of the oven and preheat the oven to 350 degrees F. In a large bowl, combine the ground chicken, veal and pork with the onion mixture, bread crumbs, buttermilk, eggs, salt and pepper and blend well. Transfer the meat mixture to 9-by-5-by-3-inch loaf pan, mounding it slightly; smooth the top with the back of a spoon.

3. Bake the meat loaf for about 1¼ hours, or until an instant-reading thermometer inserted into the center of the loaf barely registers 145 degrees F. Let the loaf stand on a rack for 10 minutes before slicing. Serve hot.

Lemon Green Beans

Serves 6 to 8

If your garden (or your greengrocer) supplies you with the ultra skinny green beanlets called *haricots verts*, this dish will be particularly eye-appealing and interesting.

2 pounds green beans or *haricots verts*, trimmed if
    necessary, the larger beans cut into 1½-inch
    pieces
½ stick (4 tablespoons) unsalted butter
¼ cup olive oil
Finely grated zest (colored peel) of 2 large lemons
¾ teaspoon salt
½ teaspoon freshly ground black pepper

1. Bring a large pan of lightly salted water to a boil over high heat. Add the beans and cook, stirring once or twice, until just tender, 5 minutes for regular beans, 2 minutes for *haricots verts*. Drain and transfer to a large bowl of very cold water. Cool completely and drain well. *The beans can be prepared to this point 1 day ahead. Wrap well and refrigerate.*

2. In a large skillet, melt the butter in the olive oil over medium heat. Add the beans and cook, tossing and stirring occasionally, until heated through, 4 to 5 minutes. Stir in the lemon zest, salt and pepper. Serve hot.

Finishing touches: Serve the meat loaf and green beans with Classic Scalloped Spuds (page 127) or Sally Schneider's Amazing Buttermilk Mashed Potatoes (page 123). Accompany the meal with crusty baguettes and sweet butter and drink a chilled, crisp white wine, such as a Sauvignon blanc. For dessert, nibble strawberries or other fresh fruit from the garden.

Leftovers: Slice the meat loaf very thin and serve it atop a big green salad, tossed with freshly made croutons and dressed with red wine vinegar and olive oil.

Glazed Ham and Carrot Mosaic Loaf

Serves 6 to 8

This meat loaf is generously spangled with diced ham and carrots and piquantly glazed with hot pepper jelly. It's eye appealing, and the flavor combination is unexpectedly harmonious. The better the ham you use (firm, lean, smoky), the better the meat loaf.

3 large carrots (about ¾ pound), peeled and cut into
    ¼-inch dice
½ stick (4 tablespoons) unsalted butter
2 cups finely chopped onions
½ pound baked ham, trimmed of fat and cut into ¼-
    inch dice
1 pound ground beef
½ pound ground pork
½ pound ground veal
2 eggs, beaten
½ cup corn flake crumbs
2 teaspoons salt
1 teaspoon freshly ground black pepper
⅔ cup hot pepper jelly

1. Bring a pot of lightly salted water to a boil. Add the carrots and cook, stirring once or twice, until just tender, about 5 minutes. Drain and rinse well under cold water.

2. In a large skillet, melt the butter over medium heat. When it foams, add the onions and ham, cover and cook, stirring once or twice, for 5 minutes. Add the carrots and cook uncovered, stirring once or twice, for 5 minutes longer. Remove from the heat and cool to room temperature.

3. Position a rack in the middle of the oven and preheat the oven to 350 degrees F. In a large bowl, combine the ground beef, pork and veal with the onion mixture, eggs, corn flake crumbs, salt and pepper and blend well. Transfer the meat mixture to a 9-by-5-by-3-inch loaf pan, mounding it slightly; smooth the top with the back of a spoon.

4. Bake the meat loaf for 50 minutes. Spread ⅓ cup of the pepper jelly over the loaf and bake for 20 minutes. Spread the remaining ⅓ cup pepper jelly over the loaf and bake for another 15 to 20 minutes, or until an instant-reading thermometer inserted into the center of the loaf registers 160 degrees F. Let the loaf stand on a rack for 10 minutes before slicing. Serve hot.

Sautéed Spinach

Serves 6 to 8

This spinach cooks in nothing more than a bit of butter and onion and the steam created by the water clinging to the tender, green leaves. Salt, pepper and a pinch of nutmeg are the only seasonings, and the resulting intense spinach flavor is the perfect accompaniment to the carrot-sweet, ham-smoky meat loaf. Serve the spinach beside the loaf and consider spooning the pale green pan juices over mashed potatoes. This sounds like a titanic amount of spinach, but the leaves wilt down considerably.

¾ stick (6 tablespoons) unsalted butter
1 cup grated onion
6 large bunches flat-leaf spinach (about 4 pounds), stems removed, well-rinsed, with clinging moisture
1½ teaspoons salt
¾ teaspoon freshly ground black pepper
¼ teaspoon freshly grated nutmeg

1. In a large nonreactive flameproof casserole, melt the butter over low heat. Add the onion, cover and cook, stirring once or twice, until softened and translucent, about 5 minutes; do not brown.

2. Raise the heat to medium-high. Add a large handful of the spinach to the skillet and cook, turning and stirring the leaves with a pair of large spoons. As the spinach wilts, add another large handful of leaves. Continue to cook and stir, always adding fresh spinach as that in the pan wilts down.

3. When all the spinach has cooked down (about 6 minutes total time), season with the salt, pepper and nutmeg. Serve the spinach along with any juices in the pan immediately.

■ ■ ■

Finishing touches: Accompany the meat loaf and spinach with The Mashed Potatoes (page 75), Sally Schneider's Amazing Buttermilk Mashed Potatoes (page 123) or Shiitake Mushroom Rice (page 117). Drink a spicy red wine, such as zinfandel. Dessert might be something featuring nuts—old-fashioned pecan pie, for example.

Leftovers: Wrap sliced meat loaf, topped with slices of sharp cheddar cheese, in foil and oven warm. Serve with a spinach salad.

The Dream Loaf

Serves 6 to 8

I would be remiss if somewhere in this collection of superlative meat loaves I didn't include one that is what I think of as the best of the best. My lengthy (and pleasurable) researches into what separates the merely good meat loaves from the magnificent ones have lead me to certain conclusions about those ingredients without which, I believe, no loaf can hope to achieve greatness. It is these essential ingredients that I have jam-packed into one loaf: The Dream Loaf, the quintessential meat loaf and the ultimate expression of the entire genre. If there is a better meat loaf in the galaxy, beings from that lucky planet have yet to make contact with those of us here on Earth. So, until then, eat this.

½ stick (4 tablespoons) unsalted butter
1¼ cups finely chopped onions
1 medium red bell pepper, finely chopped (about 1 cup)
¼ cup sliced green onion
2 garlic cloves, minced
2 eggs, beaten
⅓ cup canned beef broth
1 tablespoon Worcestershire sauce
1 tablespoon hot pepper sauce (preferably Trappey's Red Devil)

1 tablespoon soy sauce
1 pound ground beef
½ pound ground pork
½ pound ground veal
4 ounces Monterey Jack cheese, grated (about 1 cup)
¾ cup saltine cracker crumbs
½ cup ketchup
5 slices of thick-cut bacon, halved crosswise

1. In a large skillet, melt the butter over medium heat. When it foams, add the onions, bell pepper, green onion and garlic. Cover and cook for 5 minutes. Uncover and cook, stirring often, for another 4 to 5 minutes, or until the vegetables are lightly browned. Remove from the heat and cool to room temperature.

2. Position a rack in the middle of the oven and preheat the oven to 350 degrees F. In a medium bowl, whisk together the eggs, beef broth, Worcestershire sauce, pepper sauce and soy sauce until well blended. In a large bowl, combine the ground beef, pork and veal with the onion mixture, the egg mixture, cheese and cracker crumbs. Mix lightly but thoroughly. Transfer the meat mixture to a shallow baking dish and shape it into a loaf about 3 inches thick; smooth the top with the back of a spoon. Spread the ketchup evenly over the loaf. Arrange the bacon strips atop the ketchup, overlapping them slightly if necessary.

3. Bake for about 1½ hours, or until an instant-reading thermometer inserted into the center of the loaf registers 160 degrees F. Let the loaf stand on a rack for 10 minutes before slicing.

The Mashed Potatoes

Serves 6 to 8

The ultimate meat loaf deserves the ultimate in mashed potatoes; hence this recipe. While it's hard for me to play favorites among mashed potato recipes (as long as they're not from a box, I never met a mashed spud I couldn't get somewhat affectionate for), I will allow that this one produces potatoes that are the richest, silkiest and creamiest. If these are your mashed potato standards, too, then you'll enjoy the following as much as I do.

4½ pounds russet baking potatoes (8 to 9 large),
 peeled and chunked
1¼ cups milk
2 teaspoons salt
1 cup (8 ounces) sour cream, at room temperature
1 teaspoon freshly ground black pepper
Unsalted butter, as accompaniment (optional)

1. Put the potatoes in a large saucepan with cold, lightly salted water. Set over medium heat and bring to a boil. Lower the heat slightly and cook uncovered, stirring once or twice, until the potatoes are very tender, about 25 minutes.

2. Meanwhile, in a small saucepan, combine the milk and the salt and bring just to a simmer over low heat. Drain the potatoes and force them through the medium disk of a food mill or through a ricer or mash them by hand; do not use a food processor. Return the potatoes to their pan and set over low heat. Stir the potatoes constantly for 3 minutes. Slowly whisk in the hot milk, then beat in the sour cream. Beat the potatoes for a minute or two, until they are fluffy. Stir in the pepper and serve hot, passing butter at the table if desired.

■ ■ ■

Finishing touches: The perfect meat loaf and the ultimate mashed potatoes deserve the best possible side accompaniment. Creamed Fresh Corn (page 17), Well-Cheddared Broccoli (page 79) or Harvard Beets (page 27) would all make fine partners, and I for one would be hard-pressed to choose. Garlic bread (good bread, real butter, fresh garlic) would round things out nicely, and I would drink Carlsberg Elephant Beer. Since this is turning out to be My Favorite Meal, I'd also serve my favorite dessert: rhubarb pie.

Leftovers: Wrap the meat loaf in foil, oven warm it and serve it napped with heated leftover creamed corn.

Chapter Four

MEAT LOAVES OF THE RICH AND FAMOUS

Recipes from the Celebrated

The rich and famous are not like you and me. They have someone to make their meat loaves for them—not to mention shop for, serve forth, and clean up after. With our hands deep in a sink of soapy water, scraping futilely at those last, stubborn burnt-on bits at the bottom of the meat loaf baking dish, it would be entirely human of us to speculate that removed as they are from the joys of the creative process, the rich and famous do not have meat loaves that taste as good as ours do. This, however, would be a mistake. In fact, meat loaves taste just as good *when the chopping, sweating, serving and scrubbing are left to someone else, and the meat loves of the R & F are perfectly delicious, as the following collection will illustrate. You may eat these off of Melmac instead of Minton, wash them down with beer instead of Bordeaux and you will almost certainly have to do the dishes yourself, but otherwise the good life is waiting for you at the end of a (stainless steel) fork.* Bon appétit!

Ann Landers's Good Advice Meat Loaf

Serves 6 to 8

Ann Landers, America's doyenne of sound advice, printed this recipe years ago and still gets regular reader requests for a copy. Various versions of the loaf are attributed to the columnist, but this one is official. Like many a fine-tuned formula, the recipe is brand name specific, and the results are as reliable as Ann herself. Neither she nor I make any claim that this recipe will fix your ailing marriage, calm your angry mother-in-law or get your boss off your back, but it will solve the problems of what to make for dinner tonight. The bacon, by the way, is optional. "Use it," says Miss Landers, "if you like that flavor."

¾ cup ketchup
½ cup warm water
2 eggs, beaten
1 envelope Lipton Onion Recipe Soup Mix
1 teaspoon Accent
2 pounds ground beef
1½ cups fine, dry bread crumbs
1 can (8 ounces) Hunt's tomato sauce
2 slices of bacon, halved crosswise (optional)

1. Position a rack in the middle of the oven and preheat the oven to 350 degrees F. In a medium bowl, whisk together the ketchup, water, eggs, soup mix and Accent. In a large bowl, crumble the beef. Add the ketchup mixture and bread crumbs and mix thoroughly. Transfer the meat mixture to a 9-by-5-by-3-inch loaf pan, mounding it slightly. Pour the tomato sauce over the loaf. If you are using them, arrange the bacon strips atop the sauce.

2. Bake the meat loaf for about 1 hour, or until an instant-reading thermometer inserted into the center of the loaf registers 145 degrees F. Let the loaf rest on a rack for 10 minutes before slicing.

Well-Cheddared Broccoli

Serves 6 to 8

Plenty of cheddar cheese is one way to get broccoli doubters interested in eating their vegetables. Another way to gain converts is to begin with fresh broccoli and cook it only for the minimum amount of time, thus avoiding both the strong flavor and mushy texture that put some people off. There is a generous amount of cheese sauce here, some of which will inevitably end up on your meat loaf, making an already good thing that much better.

9 cups broccoli florets (from about 3 medium
    bunches)
2 teaspoons salt
2 cans (11 ounces each) condensed cheddar cheese
    soup/sauce
¾ cup evaporated milk
3 teaspoons hot pepper sauce
8 ounces sharp cheddar cheese, grated (about 2 cups)

1. Bring a large pot of water to a boil. Add the broccoli florets and salt and cook, stirring once or twice, for 4 minutes (the water need not even return to the boil). Drain the broccoli into a colander and rinse under cold running water until cool; drain well. *The broccoli can be prepared to this point up to 1 day ahead. Wrap well and refrigerate.*

2. In a large saucepan, whisk together the cheese soup/sauce, evaporated milk and hot pepper sauce. Warm over low heat until steaming. Stir in the broccoli and grated cheese and cook, partially covered, stirring often, until the broccoli is just heated through and the cheese melts, about 5 minutes. Adjust the seasoning and serve hot.

■ ■ ■

Finishing touches: Serve this meat loaf and the broccoli with mashed potatoes, hot biscuits and homemade preserves. Drink a tall glass of real iced tea and serve warm chocolate chip cookies and cold milk for dessert.

Leftovers: This basic meat loaf is simply wonderful as a lunch box sandwich. Slice it, arrange the slices on whole wheat bread and spread, just before eating, with good, sharp mustard.

The El Paso Chile Company's Tex-Mex Meat Loaf

Serves 8

As intensely flavorful and fiery as a bowl of good chili (only sliceable), the Southwestern meat loaf is the work of Park and Norma Kerr, the Texas-based owners of a premium sales company. They report that El Pasoans like things very hot, but suggest that the number of jalapeños can be adjusted to avoid actually scorching your tongue. Even with no chiles at all (crazy talk, I know), this is one meat loaf that will never be called bland.

3 tablespoons olive oil
1 cup finely chopped onion
1 large, heavy red bell pepper, finely chopped
2 to 3 fresh jalapeño chiles, stemmed and minced
2 garlic cloves, minced
2 tablespoons chili powder blend
2 teaspoons salt
1½ teaspoons dried oregano, crumbled
1½ teaspoons ground cumin
1 can (28 ounces) Italian-style plum tomatoes, crushed and drained
1½ pounds ground beef
½ pound ground pork
1 cup fine, dry bread crumbs
2 eggs, beaten
1 cup canned or defrosted corn kernels, well drained
3 green onions, sliced
8 ounces medium-sharp cheddar cheese, grated (about 2 cups)

1. In a large nonreactive skillet, warm the olive oil over medium heat. Add the onion, red bell pepper, jalapeños, garlic, chili powder, salt, oregano and cumin. Cover and cook, stirring once or twice, for 10 minutes. Add the tomatoes and cook covered, stirring once or twice, for 10 minutes. Remove from the heat and cool to room temperature.

2. Position a rack in the middle of the oven and preheat the oven to 350 degrees F. In a large bowl, combine the ground beef and pork with the tomato mixture, bread crumbs, eggs, corn and green onions and mix well. Transfer the meat mixture to a shallow baking dish and form it into a flat loaf about 2½ inches thick; smooth the top with the back of a spoon. Bake for about 1 hour and 20 minutes, or until an instant-reading thermometer inserted into the center of the loaf registers 160 degrees F.

3. Pour off any drippings from the dish. Sprinkle the cheese evenly over the meat loaf and return it to the oven until the cheese just melts, about 4 minutes. Let the meat loaf rest for 10 minutes before slicing. Serve hot.

Rio Grande Pilaf

Serves 8

This easy side dish is just Spanish rice with an attitude. The heat level of the bottled salsa you choose will determine the heat level of the finished rice. Pinto beans, red kidney beans or chick-peas can be substituted for the black beans, and the cilantro (though I think it makes the rice special) is optional.

3 tablespoons olive oil
½ cup finely chopped onion
2 garlic cloves, minced
½ teaspoon dried oregano, crumbled
½ teaspoon ground cumin
1 cup long-grain white rice
1½ cups chicken stock or canned broth
¾ cup tomato-based bottled salsa
1 teaspoon salt
1 can (16 ounces) black beans, rinsed and drained
⅓ cup finely chopped fresh cilantro (optional)

1. In a medium nonreactive saucepan, warm the olive oil over low heat. Stir in the onion, garlic, oregano and cumin, cover and cook, stirring once or twice, for 10 minutes. Add the rice and cook, stirring often, for 3 minutes, or until the grains are fully coated with oil and turn slightly translucent. Stir in the broth, salsa and salt. Raise the heat, bring the liquid to a boil, then lower the heat. Cover the pan and simmer undisturbed for 20 minutes.

2. Add the beans to the pan, spreading them atop the rice, cover and cook for another 2 minutes. Remove the pan from the heat and let stand for 5 minutes. Sprinkle the cilantro over the beans and stir them into the rice. Serve hot.

■ ■ ■

Finishing touches: Serve the meat loaf and rice with a simple green vegetable, such as sautéed zucchini, and accompany the meal with warmed flour tortillas or corn bread. Drink a cold Mexican beer, like Dos Equis or Bohemia. Serve chilled fresh citrus fruit for dessert.

Leftovers: Oven warm thin slices of meat loaf wrapped in foil. Arrange them on a split hard roll. Top with thin slices of peeled avocado and juicy tomato.

Paul Prudhomme's Cajun Meat Loaf

Serves 6 to 8

When meat loaf mavens taste this loaf they praise the Louisiana chef's technique of layering flavors, building the taste and heat level gradually to the point just before things get too hot. They shake their heads in admiration at the spicy balancing act and look regretfully at the portion rapidly vanishing from their plates; their eyes grow moist. Are they lamenting another Prudhomme meat loaf that never made it to the leftover stage, or is it just the cayenne, hot sauce, white pepper and black pepper combusting on their tongues? Here, to help you decide for yourself, is the recipe for the legendary loaf, adapted slightly from *Chef Paul Prudhomme's Louisiana Kitchen*.

½ stick (4 tablespoons) unsalted butter
¾ cup finely chopped onion
½ cup finely chopped celery
½ cup finely chopped red bell pepper
¼ cup sliced green onions
3 garlic cloves, minced
1 tablespoon hot pepper sauce
1 tablespoon Worcestershire sauce
1 tablespoon salt
1 teaspoon cayenne pepper
1 teaspoon dried thyme leaves, crumbled
1 teaspoon freshly ground black pepper
½ teaspoon freshly ground white pepper
½ teaspoon ground cumin
½ teaspoon freshly grated nutmeg
½ cup whipping cream or heavy cream
½ cup ketchup
1 pound ground beef
½ pound ground pork
½ pound ground veal
2 eggs, beaten
1 cup fine, dry bread crumbs

1. In a medium nonreactive saucepan, melt the butter over medium heat. When it foams, add the onion, celery, red bell pepper, green onions, garlic, hot pepper sauce, Worcestershire sauce, salt, cayenne, thyme, black pepper, white pepper, cumin and nutmeg. Cook, stirring often and scraping the bottom of the pan, until the mixture begins to stick, about 6 minutes. Stir in the cream and ketchup and continue to cook for another 2 minutes. Remove from the heat and cool to room temperature.

2. Position a rack in the middle of the oven and preheat the oven to 350 degrees F. In a large bowl, combine the ground beef, pork and veal with the onion mixture, eggs and bread crumbs and mix thoroughly. Transfer the mixture to a shallow baking dish and shape it into a flat loaf about 2½ inches thick; smooth the top.

3. Bake for 25 minutes, then raise the oven temperature to 400 degrees F. and bake for 35 minutes longer, or until an instant-reading thermometer inserted into the center of the loaf registers 160 degrees F. Let the loaf rest on a rack for 10 minutes before slicing. Serve hot.

Baked Cheese Grits with Hot Sausage and Onions

Serves 6 to 8

People dislike hominy grits, a meal ground from dried corn, because it is so bland, I think, which explains why it is flavored up so many ways. In this hot and gooey casserole, spicy sausage, green onions and two kinds of cheese transform simple (bland) grits into a rich and satisfying side dish, worthy of sharing the plate with a legendary, Louisiana meat loaf. If the smoked, spiced Cajun sausage called andouille is unavailable to you, Hillshire Farms Hot Links, available in many supermarkets, can be substituted.

3 tablespoons olive oil
½ pound andouille or other hot, smoked sausage, cut into ¼-inch dice
⅔ cup sliced green onions
4 cups chicken stock or canned broth
1 cup regular cooking (not instant) white hominy grits
½ teaspoon freshly ground black pepper
3 eggs, beaten
4 ounces sharp cheddar cheese, shredded (about 1 cup)
4 ounces Monterey Jack cheese, shredded (about 1 cup)

1. Position a rack in the middle of the oven and preheat the oven to 350 degrees F. Butter a 2½-quart baking dish. In a large saucepan, warm the olive oil over medium heat. Add the diced sausage and cook uncovered, stirring once or twice, for 7 minutes, or until lightly browned. Add the green onions and cook, stirring often, for 3 minutes, or until the sausage is lightly browned.

2. Add the chicken stock and bring it to a boil. Slowly stir in the grits and pepper. Bring to a boil, then lower the heat and cook partially covered, stirring often, for about 20 minutes, or until the grits mixture is very thick. Remove from the heat.

3. In a medium bowl, whisk 1 cup of the hot grits into the beaten eggs. Slowly stir this mixture back into the grits. Stir in the cheeses. Transfer the grits to the prepared baking dish.

4. Bake for about 40 minutes, or until golden brown and lightly set. Let the casserole rest on a rack for 5 minutes before serving.

■ ■ ■

Finishing touches: Serve the meat loaf and grits with a plain green vegetable, like sautéed zucchini, and accompany the meal with hot corn bread, butter and honey. Drink an ice cold beer (or two). For dessert, serve pecan pie or bread pudding.

Leftovers: A meat loaf this good makes a spectacular leftover. I like it on a sandwich of leftover corn bread, enjoyed with a glass of cold milk and eaten late at night, by the light of an open refrigerator door.

Good Enough To Eat's Upper West Side Meat Loaf

Serves 10 to 12

Good Enough To Eat is both a charming Manhattan restaurant highly esteemed for its homey fare and the undiscovered gem of a cookbook based on the restaurant's menu. Among the best of co-owners Carrie Levin and Ann Nickinson's dishes is the famous meat loaf, a dish so good Carrie actually served it at her wedding. It's richly flavored and moist, and its party-size proportions mean it either feeds a modest crowd or leaves the cook with plenty of savory leftovers.

¾ stick (6 tablespoons) unsalted butter, or ⅓ cup rendered bacon fat
4 cups finely chopped onions
¾ pound mushrooms, coarsely chopped
2 medium green bell peppers, finely chopped (about 2 cups)
1 cup finely chopped celery
2 garlic cloves, minced
1½ teaspoons dried basil, crumbled
1½ teaspoons dried oregano, crumbled
3 teaspoons salt
2 pounds ground beef
1 pound ground veal
1 pound ground pork
1¼ cups fine, dry bread crumbs
1 can (10¾ ounces) tomato soup
¾ cup ketchup
2 eggs, beaten
¼ cup grated Parmesan cheese
¼ cup finely chopped flat-leaf parsley
1 tablespoon mayonnaise
1 tablespoon tomato paste
2 teaspoons Worcestershire sauce
2 teaspoons freshly ground black pepper
½ teaspoon sweet paprika
8 slices of bacon, halved crosswise

1. In a large skillet, melt the butter over medium heat. When it foams, add the onions, mushrooms, bell peppers, celery, garlic, basil, oregano and 1 teaspoon of the salt. Cover and cook, stirring once or twice, for 10 minutes. Cool to room temperature.

2. Position a rack in the middle of the oven and preheat the oven to 400 degrees F. In a very large bowl, combine the onion mixture and the remaining ingredients except the bacon and mix thoroughly. Divide the meat mixture in half and on a large, shallow baking sheet, form each half into a 5-by-10-inch rectangular loaf. Arrange the bacon strips atop the loaves, overlapping them slightly.

3. Bake the loaves for 15 minutes, then lower the oven temperature to 350 degrees F. and bake for 40 to 50 minutes longer, or until an instant-reading thermometer inserted into the center of a loaf registers 160 degrees F. Let the loaves rest for 10 minutes on a rack before slicing. Serve hot.

Easy Macaroni and Cheese for a Crowd

Serves 10 to 12

Although Good Enough To Eat now serves classic mashed potatoes with its meat loaf, in the old days the starch on the side was macaroni and cheese, and the combination is a good one, still preferred by many restaurateurs unwilling to go through the constant maneuvering needed to produce hot, fluffy mashed potatoes throughout a busy evening for service. Here's an easy, basic mac 'n' cheese that is simple enough to serve as a side dish, but tasty enough to stand alone as a main course. Buttering the baking dish insures a crisp, chewy brown bottom crust—possibly the best part of this entire enterprise.

1½ pounds dried pasta elbow twists
2 cans (12 ounces each) evaporated milk
2 tablespoons hot pepper sauce
1 pound sharp cheddar cheese, grated (about 4 cups)
8 ounces Monterey Jack cheese, grated (about 2 cups)
1 cup freshly grated Parmesan cheese (about 4
   ounces)
½ cup soft, fresh bread crumbs
½ stick (4 tablespoons) unsalted butter, melted

1. Position a rack in the middle of the oven and preheat the oven to 400 degrees F. Butter a shallow 4½-quart baking dish. Bring a very large pot of salted water to a boil. Stir in the pasta and cook, stirring once or twice, until the pasta is just tender, about 9 minutes. Drain well; do not rinse with cold water.

2. Meanwhile, in a small saucepan, combine the evaporated milk and hot pepper sauce and bring just to a simmer over low heat. Return the hot, drained pasta to the pot in which it was cooked. Stir in the evaporated milk mixture. Gradually add the cheddar and Monterey Jack cheeses and ½ cup of the Parmesan, stirring to prevent clumps. Transfer the pasta mixture to the prepared baking dish. In a small bowl, mix together the remaining ½ cup Parmesan cheese and the bread crumbs. Sprinkle evenly over the top of the pasta. Drizzle the melted butter over the crumb mixture.

3. Bake for about 30 minutes, or until the cheeses are melted and the top of the casserole is lightly browned. Let rest for at least 5 minutes before serving. Serve hot or warm.

■ ■ ■

Finishing touches: Accompany the meat loaf and macaroni with fresh spinach sautéed in butter. Offer warmed ketchup or chili sauce as an optional condiment, serve soft dinner rolls and drink a fruity, medium-bodied red wine—like a Beaujolais—or a cold beer. Dessert should be something homey. If you locate a copy of Carrie and Ann's book, try their spectacular Devil's Food Chocolate Cake.

Leftovers: Slice leftover meat loaf, layer it over leftover macaroni, cover and oven warm until just heated through. Serve with ketchup.

Rick Rodgers's Ballpark Meat Loaf

Serves 8 to 10

Rick Rodgers is the maestro of mince: he's the author of *365 Ways to Cook Hamburger and Other Ground Meats* and the creator of an astonishing number of admirable meat loaves. Among the best of them is Ground Meat Recipe Number 69, which includes a big-league measure of ballpark mustard and sweet pickle relish, effectively and deliciously combining America's favorite pastime with America's favorite suppertime treat.

⅔ cup plus 2 tablespoons spicy brown mustard
1 cup sweet pickle relish with juices
1½ cups soft, fresh bread crumbs
2 eggs, beaten
2 cups finely chopped onions
2 teaspoons garlic salt
¼ teaspoon freshly ground black pepper
1½ pounds ground beef
1½ pounds ground pork
1 tablespoon packed light brown sugar

1. Position a rack in the middle of the oven and preheat the oven to 350 degrees F. In a large bowl, combine ⅔ cup of the mustard, the pickle relish, bread crumbs, eggs, onions, garlic salt and pepper and mix to blend well. Add the ground beef and pork and mix until combined. Divide the mixture between two 8-by-4-by-2½-inch loaf pans, mounding it slightly.

2. Bake for about 40 minutes, or until an instant-reading thermometer inserted into the center of the loaf registers 160 degrees F. In a small bowl, whisk together the remaining 2 tablespoons mustard and the brown sugar. Brush the mixture evenly over the top of the meat loaves and bake until the topping is glazed, about 5 minutes. Let the loaves rest on a rack for 10 minutes before slicing.

Hot and Smoky Baked Beans

Serves 8 to 10

These slightly fiery baked beans can be served the day they're baked (they are best warm, not hot) or they can be completed one day in advance and reheated.

3½ cups (about 1 pound, 7 ounces) dried Great Northern white beans, picked over
1 smoked ham hock
3½ teaspoons salt
2 cups finely chopped onions
1¼ cups prepared, tomato-based barbecue sauce
1¼ cups prepared, tomato-based hot salsa
⅓ cup packed light brown sugar
¼ cup Dijon-style mustard
¼ cup unsulphured molasses

1. In a 5-quart pan combine the beans with cold water to cover them generously. Set over medium heat and bring to a full boil. Remove the pan from the heat and let the beans stand in the water until cool.

2. Drain, again cover the beans generously with cold water and set the pan over medium heat. Add the ham hock to the pan and bring the water to a boil. Lower the heat and simmer, uncovered, stirring once or twice, for 20 minutes. Stir in 2 teaspoons of the salt and cook for another 15 to 20 minutes, or until the beans are tender. Remove and reserve the ham hock. Drain the beans, reserving 1½ cups of the cooking water.

3. Position a rack in the middle of the oven and preheat the oven to 350 degrees F. In a large bowl, stir together the beans, reserved bean cooking water, onions, barbecue sauce, salsa, brown sugar, mustard, molasses and the remaining 1½ teaspoons salt. Transfer the mixture to a deep, 4½- to 5-quart ovenproof casserole or bean pot. Bury the ham hock in the middle of the beans and bake uncovered for 1 hour. Stir the beans and bake for another 30 to 40 minutes, or until very thick but not dry. Remove and discard the ham hock before serving. Serve warm.

■ ■ ■

Finishing touches: Working with the ballpark theme, I would serve the meat loaf and baked beans with peanuts in the shell, coleslaw and even hot dog buns, toasted. Drink cold beer or a tall soft drink and for dessert, offer Cracker Jacks or homemade sno-cones.

Leftovers: Cut the meat loaf into narrow slices, wrap in foil and oven warm. Serve on hot dog buns with ketchup, mustard and onions.

Ed Debevic's Burnt Diner Meat Loaf

Serves 8 to 10

At Ed Debevic's the Fifties concept diners variously located in cities such as Chicago, Los Angeles, New York and Osaka, there is no Ed, but there is meat loaf, and a very good one it is, too. Lavishly iced with tomato paste, which chars lightly during baking, it is called "burnt," which should in no way lead you to think of post-honeymoon kitchen disasters. At Ed's, the loaves are baked one day ahead, mellowing the flavors, and then reheated for serving. Pork can replace some of the beef, if you wish.

3 tablespoons olive oil
1½ cups finely chopped onions
1 large, heavy red bell pepper, finely chopped (about 1½ cups)
5 garlic cloves, minced
3 eggs
⅓ cup whipping cream or heavy cream
2½ tablespoons soy sauce
1½ teaspoons salt
1 teaspoon freshly ground black pepper
3 pounds ground beef
1½ cups fine, dry, seasoned bread crumbs
½ cup tomato paste

1. In a large skillet, warm the olive oil over medium-high heat. Add the onions, bell pepper and garlic and cook, tossing and stirring, for 5 minutes. Remove from the heat and cool to room temperature.

2. Position a rack in the middle of the oven and preheat the oven to 325 degrees F. In a medium bowl, whisk together the eggs, cream, soy sauce, salt and pepper. Crumble the beef into a large bowl. Add the egg mixture and partially combine. Add the onion-bell pepper mixture and bread crumbs and combine lightly but thoroughly. Pack the meat mixture into a 9-by-5-by-3-inch loaf pan, mounding it slightly; smooth the top with the back of a spoon. Spread the tomato paste in an even layer over the top of the loaf.

3. Bake for about 2 hours, or until the top of the loaf is lightly blackened and an instant-reading thermometer inserted into the center of the loaf registers 145 degrees F. Let stand on a rack for 10 minutes before slicing. Serve hot. *The loaf can be prepared 1 day ahead. Wrap and refrigerate. Slice the loaf, wrap each slice individually in plastic and reheat in a microwave oven or wrap in foil and rewarm in a preheated 400 degree F. conventional oven for about 20 minutes.*

Ed's Caramelized Onion Stuff

Makes about 3 cups

Ed Debevic's meat loaf becomes really special when served with a generous dollop of this intensely caramelized onion relish—a condiment that could well knock thoughts of ketchup right off your plate. Though the cooking process takes awhile, it's not complicated and, like Ed's meat loaf, it can be completed a day in advance and reheated just before serving time. (Kitchen tip: Chilling the onions before peeling and slicing them will prevent—or at least reduce—eye discomfort and tears.)

¾ stick (6 tablespoons) unsalted butter
2 tablespoons corn oil
3½ pounds onions (4 very large), peeled and very
    thinly sliced (about 14 cups)
1 cup water
⅓ cup sugar
½ teaspoon salt

1. In a heavy, deep skillet or large flameproof casserole melt the butter in the oil over medium heat. Stir in the onions, cover and cook, stirring once or twice, for 10 minutes, or until the onions are limp and have colored slightly.

2. Raise the heat and cook, stirring often, until the onion juices are beginning to brown on the bottom and sides of the skillet, about 10 minutes. Stir in ⅓ cup of the water and cook uncovered, scraping occasionally to dissolve the browned juices, about 5 minutes. Stir in another ⅓ cup water and continue to cook and to scrape the pan for 5 minutes. Add the remaining ⅓ cup water, the sugar and salt and cook, continuing to scrape the pan occasionally, for another 5 minutes, or until the onions are very brown, have reduced to about 3 cups and the sides and bottom of the pan are clear of caramelized onion juices. *The onion stuff can be prepared up to 3 days ahead. Cool to room temperature and refrigerate, covered. Rewarm in a heavy saucepan over low heat, or in a microwave oven.*

3. Serve hot, dolloped atop slices of Ed's meat loaf.

■ ■ ■

Finishing touches: Serve the meat loaf and its caramelized onion garnish with Classic Scalloped Spuds (page 127) and Creamed Peas and Carrots (page 99). Drink a vanilla milk shake or iced tea. Suitable diner desserts might be tapioca pudding or warm cherry pie à la mode.

Leftovers: Spread a slice of meat loaf with some of the onion stuff. Lay a slice of Swiss or cheddar cheese over the onions, wrap in foil and oven warm until heated through and the cheese melts.

Serendipity 3's Country Meat Loaf

Serves 8 to 10

Serendipity 3 is a New York City institution. Located on the Upper East Side, hard by Bloomingdale's, this ice cream parlor slash gift shoppe has served as a watering hole for well-to-do bargain hunters and their well-to-do offspring for years. In fact, kids of all ages are made welcome here, and despite the general white-tile-and-bentwood atmosphere, there's more than ice cream to be enjoyed at Serendipity 3. I can recall an exemplary bowl of chili, for example, and on Tuesdays the blue plate special is an excellent meat loaf, complete with peas and carrots, mashed potatoes and Jell-O for dessert. Like everything else about Serendipity 3, trappings such as Jell-O camouflage an underlying seriousness of intent that always takes me by surprise. Though served with brown mushroom gravy at the restaurant, this loaf is wonderful just as it comes from the oven.

2 eggs
2 cups canned beef broth or bouillon
1 cup ketchup
½ cup finely chopped flat-leaf parsley
2 tablespoons Dijon-style mustard
2 teaspoons dried rosemary, crumbled
2 teaspoons freshly ground black pepper
1¾ teaspoons garlic powder
1½ teaspoons salt
2 cups finely chopped onions
1 large, heavy red bell pepper, finely chopped (about 1½ cups)
1 cup finely chopped celery
3 ounces medium-sharp cheddar cheese, grated (about ¾ cup)
2½ pounds ground beef
1 cup fine, dry, seasoned bread crumbs

1. Position a rack in the middle of the oven and preheat the oven to 375 degrees F. In a medium bowl, whisk the eggs. Whisk in the beef bouillon, ketchup, parsley, mustard, rosemary, pepper, garlic powder and salt. Stir in the onions, red bell pepper, celery and cheese. In a large bowl, crumble the ground beef. Add the egg mixture and bread crumbs and mix gently but thoroughly. Transfer the meat mixture to a shallow baking dish and shape it into a flat loaf about 2½ inches thick; smooth the top with the back of a spoon.

2. Bake for about 1¼ hours, or until the loaf is crusty and well-browned and an instant-reading thermometer inserted into the center of the loaf registers 145 degrees F. Let stand on a rack for 10 minutes before slicing.

Sweet Potato Fries

Serves 8 to 10

When you can bear to serve a starch other than mashed potatoes with your meat loaf, consider these habit-forming fries. They're just as easy to make as the regular sort, but the color and flavor are a refreshing change of pace. Adults will enjoy them with no more than a sprinkle of salt and pepper, while kids (possibly some adults, too) will dunk them in ketchup.

About 2 quarts corn oil, for deep-frying
4½ pounds sweet potatoes (5 or 6 large), peeled and
      cut into thin rounds
Coarse (kosher) salt and freshly ground black pepper

1. In a deep-fryer or heavy 5-quart kettle, warm the corn oil over medium heat to 375 degrees F. The oil should fill the fryer or kettle no more than halfway.

2. Add a modest handful of the sweet potatoes to the hot oil. The oil will bubble furiously, then subside to a brisk simmer; if it shows signs of boiling over, stir it down with a heavy metal spoon. Cook the potatoes, stirring occasionally, until they are lightly browned and crisp around the edges, about 6 minutes. With a slotted spoon, transfer the fried potatoes to absorbent paper. Sprinkle with salt and pepper to taste. Repeat with the remaining potatoes, letting the oil return to 375 degrees F

between batches. Serve the potatoes as you fry them, or as soon after completing the full recipe as is possible, in order that they remain crisp.

■ ■ ■

Finishing touches: Serve the meat loaf and sweet potato fries with Creamed Fresh Corn (page 17) or Creamed Peas and Carrots (page 99) and hot, flaky biscuits. For dessert, evoke Serendipity 3's famous Frozen Cappuccino by serving coffee ice cream sundaes with hot fudge sauce and whipped cream.

Leftovers: This meat loaf is excellent the next day, flavorful and moist. Try it sliced thin on a sandwich or multi-grain bread spread with just a little softened sweet butter.

Leonard Schwartz's Maple Drive and 72 Market Street Meat Loaf

Serves 8 to 10

Known as a convivial "scene" restaurant that serves atypically delicious food, 72 Market Street, in nearby Venice, has been wooing Los Angeles diners for years. Among its owners are filmmaker Tony Bill and actor Dudley Moore, who, together with executive chef Leonard Schwartz, have transferred their special brand of restaurant excitement to a new, hot hangout, Maple Drive. Both places serve memorable "best-in-town" versions of such satisfying staples as chili, crab cakes and mashed potatoes, though it is the meat loaf that has endured as the restaurant's signature dish. Like many restaurant recipes, it has been fine tuned over the years, resulting in a very precise set of instructions, which are reproduced here exactly. The precision, insists Chef Schwartz, is worth it, and I agree—this is great meat loaf.

3 tablespoons unsalted butter
¾ cup finely chopped onion
¾ cup finely chopped green onion
½ cup finely chopped carrot
¼ cup finely chopped celery
¼ cup minced red bell pepper
¼ cup minced green bell pepper
2 garlic cloves, minced
2 teaspoons salt
1 teaspoon freshly ground black pepper
1 teaspoon ground cumin
½ teaspoon freshly ground white pepper
½ teaspoon freshly grated nutmeg
¼ teaspoon cayenne pepper
½ cup ketchup
½ cup half-and-half
3 eggs, beaten
2 pounds ground beef
¾ pound bulk sausage meat (without fennel seed)
¾ cup fine, dry bread crumbs

1. In a large skillet, melt the butter over medium heat. When it foams, add the onion, green onion, carrot, celery, red bell pepper, green bell pepper and garlic. Cook, uncovered, stirring often, until the vegetables are tender and lightly colored and all moisture has evaporated, 8 to 10 minutes. Remove from the heat, cool to room temperature and refrigerate until well chilled.

2. Position a rack in the middle of the oven and preheat the oven to 375 degrees F. In a large bowl, stir together the salt, black pepper, cumin, white pepper, nutmeg and cayenne pepper. Stir in the ketchup and half-and-half and

mix thoroughly. Stir in the eggs and blend well. Crumble in the ground beef and sausage. Add the chilled vegetable mixture and bread crumbs and mix thoroughly using your hands. Knead the mixture together well for 5 minutes. Transfer the meat mixture to a baking dish and shape it into an oval loaf about 17 inches long and about 1½ inches thick. Set this baking dish into a slightly larger flameproof pan and fill the pan with enough boiling water to reach halfway up the sides of the smaller baking dish. Set this hot water bath over medium heat and return the water to a boil.

3. Set the hot water bath into the oven and bake for about 50 minutes, or until an instant-reading thermometer inserted into the center of the loaf registers 160 degrees F. Remove the baking dish from the hot water bath and let the meat loaf rest on a rack for 20 minutes before slicing. Serve hot.

Zucchini and Eggplant Fritters in Rosemary-Cornmeal Batter

Serves 8 to 10

These crunchy, batter-coated vegetable fritters are a nice contrast to the moist, tender meat loaf. I like them as is, sprinkled with a bit of coarse salt, but they're also good dipped into the Tomato-Olive Sauce (page 46) with or without the black olives. Don't substitute dried rosemary for the fresh, just omit it—the vegetables will still be good.

4 medium zucchini (about 1⅓ pounds total), scrubbed
    and trimmed
2 medium eggplants (about 2 pounds total), trimmed
⅔ cup yellow cornmeal
3 cups warm water
2½ cups unbleached all-purpose flour
3 tablespoons minced fresh rosemary
¼ teaspoon salt
About 2 quarts corn oil, for deep-frying
Coarse (kosher) salt, to taste

1. Cut the zucchini crosswise on an angle into ½-inch-thick slices. Quarter the eggplants lengthwise. Cut each quarter crosswise into ½-inch-thick pieces. Bring a large nonreactive saucepan of lightly salted water to a boil. Add the zucchini and eggplant pieces and when the water returns to a boil, cook for 1 minute, stirring once or twice. Drain and transfer the vegetables immediately to a large bowl of very cold water. Cool completely, drain well and pat dry. *The recipe can be prepared to this point several hours ahead. Cover the vegetables and hold at room temperature.*

2. Measure the cornmeal into a large bowl. Slowly whisk in the warm water. Measure the flour into a sifter; sift the flour into the cornmeal mixture, whisking constantly. Whisk in the rosemary and salt. Loosely cover and let the batter stand at room temperature for 20 minutes.

3. Meanwhile, pour 4 inches of oil into a deep-fryer or heavy, 5-quart kettle. The oil should fill the fryer or kettle no more than halfway. Warm the oil over medium heat to 375 degrees F.

4. Working in batches, drop the vegetable pieces into the batter and stir to coat. Lift each piece from the batter (fingers work best) and let some of the excess drip back into the bowl. Add the vegetables to the hot oil and fry, stirring occasionally, until crisp and golden brown, about 2 minutes. With a slotted spoon transfer the fried vegetable pieces to absorbent paper. Sprinkle lightly with coarse salt. Serve hot or warm.

■ ■ ■

Finishing touches: Serve the meat loaf and deep-fried vegetables with a creamy potato side dish—either The Mashed Potatoes (page 75) or Potatoes and Corn au Gratin (page 133). Begin the meal with a Caesar salad, pass a basket of hearty whole grain walnut bread and drink a light California red wine, like pinot noir or merlot. For dessert, serve cheesecake accompanied by a salad of marinated fresh tropical fruits—pineapple, mango, kiwi.

Leftovers: I like the loaf cold, in a sandwich of whole grain walnut bread spread with a bit of creamy goat cheese in place of mayo or ketchup.

Chapter Five

PLAYING WITH YOUR FOOD

Recipes That Entertain

Busy, busy, busy. Making meat loaf ought to be a snap (ground meat, pinch of this, can of that, mix and bake), but some cooks are constitutionally unable to leave well enough alone. Then there is the boredom theory. Studies have shown that if chimpanzees are dressed in frilly aprons and forced to bake the same meat loaf recipe over and over again, they become violent and uncooperative, first adding ingredients not on the approved list and eventually reforming and reshaping the resulting mixture into anything but a loaf. Interest-

ingly, the studies also show that the other members of the chimpanzee family group then treat this modified meat loaf as an entirely new dish, and enjoy it with apparent relish. Whether we can draw any firm conclusions from the above data remains uncertain, but we do know there are meat loaves that require more time, patience and nimbleness of finger than they ought to. Fortunately, they taste great too, as the following will illustrate.

Egg-in-the-Middle Meat Loaf

Serves 6 to 8

The only reason to tuck a row of hard-cooked eggs into the middle of a meat loaf is visual, the culinary appeal of the one-and-a-half-hour egg being nonexistent. That said, there is a certain wacky charm to finding that yellow and white bull's-eye in the center of your slice of meat loaf, and like many food whimsies, the egg doesn't actually detract from the quality of the meat loaf that surrounds it. Whether you actually eat the egg or just scoot it off to the side of your plate with the parsley is up to you.

½ stick (4 tablespoons) unsalted butter
2 cups finely chopped onions
½ cup finely chopped celery
1 pound ground beef
½ pound ground pork
½ pound ground veal
½ cup saltine cracker crumbs
2 eggs, beaten
1 tablespoon hot pepper sauce
1 tablespoon Worcestershire sauce
1½ teaspoons salt
½ teaspoon freshly ground black pepper
7 hard-cooked extra-large eggs
⅓ cup ketchup
4 slices of bacon, halved crosswise

1. In a large skillet, melt the butter over medium heat. When it foams, add the onions and celery, cover and cook, stirring once or twice, until the vegetables are lightly colored, 8 to 10 minutes. Cool to room temperature.

2. Position a rack in the middle of the oven and preheat to 350 degrees F. In a large bowl, combine the ground beef, pork and veal with the onion mixture, cracker crumbs, eggs, hot pepper sauce, Worcestershire sauce, salt and pepper and mix thoroughly. Transfer half of the mixture to a 9-by-5-by-3-inch loaf pan. With the back of a spoon, form a shallow depression in the meat mixture running the length of the pan. Trim enough white from both ends of each hard-cooked egg to reveal the yolk. Lay the eggs end to end, fitting them closely together, in the depression in the meat mixture. Top with the remaining meat mixture, sealing the ends, and mounding the meat slightly. Spread the ketchup over the top of the loaf. Lay the bacon slices, overlapping them slightly, atop the ketchup.

3. Bake the loaf about 1 hour and 20 minutes, or until an instant-reading thermometer inserted into the center of the loaf registers 160 degrees F. Let the loaf rest on a rack for 10 minutes before slicing. Serve hot.

Creamed Peas and Carrots

Serves 6 to 8

A simple cream sauce—aka white sauce—adds just the right homey note to convenient frozen peas and carrots. My version is a modern one, leaving some of the crunch in the vegetables. If you like things quieter, precook the vegetables in water and drain them before making the sauce. This can also be made with the frozen vegetable mélange of peas, carrots, corn and green beans.

3 tablespoons unsalted butter
3 tablespoons unbleached all-purpose flour
2 cups milk
⅓ cup whipping cream or heavy cream
1 teaspoon salt
½ teaspoon freshly ground pepper
⅛ teaspoon freshly grated nutmeg
4 packages (10 ounces each) frozen mixed peas and carrots, thawed and drained

1. In a large saucepan, melt the butter over low heat. When it foams, whisk in the flour and cook without browning, stirring often, for 3 minutes. Remove the pan from the heat and gradually whisk in the milk. Stir in the cream, salt, pepper, nutmeg and vegetables.

2. Set the saucepan over medium heat and bring to a simmer, stirring occasionally. Cook uncovered, stirring often, for about 5 minutes, or until the sauce thickens. Adjust the seasoning. *The vegetables can be prepared several hours ahead. Cool and hold at room temperature, rewarming them over low heat while stirring often.* Serve hot.

Finishing touches: This blue plate special cries out for plain, well-buttered mashed potatoes or Classic Scalloped Spuds (page 127). A basket of corn muffins and/or biscuits would be a fine accompaniment, as would a tall glass of real iced coffee. For dessert, offer homemade chocolate pudding, topped with a modest dollop of whipped cream.

Leftovers: Serve this meat loaf, cold, sliced thin, atop a chef's-type salad of lettuces, tomatoes and cheese, with the salad dressing of your choice.

Beef and Blue Cheese Mini-Muffin Loaves with Bacon

Serves 8 to 10

These cute meat loaves, baked in the cups of a standard muffin tin, are about the size of tennis balls. They bake fairly quickly at that size, a boon if you're in a hurry, and automatically look festive on a plate. Freezing the cheese helps keep it from melting away, though there will still be some for kitchen foragers to scrape off the pan. Hot blue cheese is pungent, which adults will like, but if you're feeding kids, consider substituting diced cheddar, which will give your loaf the more familiar ingredients of a bacon cheeseburger—and don't forget to pass the ketchup.

6 ounces good-quality blue cheese, crumbled
8 slices of bacon
1½ cups finely chopped onions
½ cup finely chopped celery
½ teaspoon dried thyme leaves, crumbled
2½ pounds ground beef
2 eggs, beaten
1 teaspoon hot pepper sauce
1 teaspoon Worcestershire sauce
½ cup fine, dry bread crumbs

1. Spread the cheese in a single layer on a small plate, cover it with plastic wrap and freeze for at least 1 hour, or until the cheese is hard.

2. Lay the bacon slices in a large skillet and set over medium-low heat. Cook, turning once or twice, until crisp, about 8 minutes. Drain the bacon on absorbent paper, cool and coarsely chop it. Pour off all but 3 tablespoons of the bacon fat in the skillet. Set the skillet over medium heat, add the onions, celery and thyme, cover and cook, stirring once or twice and scraping the bottom of the pan, for 10 minutes. Remove from the heat and cool to room temperature.

3. Position a rack in the middle of the oven and preheat the oven to 350 degrees F. In a large bowl, combine the ground beef with the onion mixture, frozen cheese, eggs, hot pepper sauce, Worcestershire sauce, bread crumbs and chopped bacon. Divide the mixture into 12 equal portions. Shape each portion into a ball (try to enclose any large nuggets of cheese completely with the meat mixture to help prevent their melting away) and place each ball in the cup of a muffin tin.

4. Bake for about 35 minutes, or until the mini-loaves are lightly browned and an instant-reading thermometer inserted into the center of a loaf registers 145 degrees F. Let the meat loaves rest on a rack for 10 minutes. Serve hot.

Cherry Tomato Sauté

Serves 8 to 10

These bright and acidy little tomatoes are the perfect accompaniment to the pungent and smoky meat loaves. If you would like to use a different fresh herb, basil, thyme or oregano would all work well here.

¾ stick (6 tablespoons) unsalted butter
⅓ cup finely chopped shallots
3 pints cherry tomatoes, stemmed and rinsed
2 tablespoons balsamic vinegar
½ teaspoon salt
½ teaspoon freshly ground black pepper
¼ cup finely chopped flat-leaf parsley

1. In a large nonreactive skillet, melt the butter over low heat. When it foams, add the shallots and cook without browning, stirring often, for 3 minutes.

2. Add the tomatoes, raise the heat slightly and cook, gently rolling the tomatoes in the hot butter, until they are just heated through, about 4 minutes.

3. Stir in the vinegar, salt and pepper. Transfer the tomatoes to a bowl, sprinkle with the parsley and serve immediately.

■ ■ ■

Finishing touches: Serve the pungent mini-loaves and tart tomatoes with mellow potatoes, such as the Classic Scalloped Spuds on page 127 or buttered mashed potatoes. Any good bread—pumpernickel, perhaps—and a dark beer, such as Anchor Steam or Double Dark Prior's, complement the meal. Dessert might be something palate-cleansing, such as fresh pineapple with a sauce of sweetened, pureed strawberries or raspberries.

Leftovers: These mini-loaves are particularly good cold, eaten as is, accompanied by a green salad, or sliced and served as a sandwich on pumpernickel bread spread with a bit of horseradish mayonnaise.

Veal Cordon Bleu Roulade

Serves 6 to 8

The combination of veal, cheese and ham that makes up the venerable culinary cliché known as veal cordon bleu brings a little country club class to ordinary meat loaf. Cooks who like things busy will be glad to know this is a roulade—with a crazy spiral of ham and Swiss cheese rolled up within. During baking, most of the cheese remains inside, but some melts out to create a deliciously gooey ooze around the sides of the loaf.

½ stick (4 tablespoons) unsalted butter
1 cup finely chopped onion
1 cup finely chopped leek (white part only)
¼ teaspoon dried thyme leaves, crumbled
1 bay leaf
1½ pounds ground veal
½ pound ground pork
2 eggs, beaten
⅔ cup soft, fresh bread crumbs
1 teaspoon salt
1 teaspoon freshly ground black pepper
8 ounces Swiss cheese, in thin slices
6 ounces boiled ham, in thin slices

1. In a large skillet, melt the butter over medium heat. When it foams, add the onion, leek, thyme and bay leaf and cook covered, stirring once or twice, until soft and translucent, 7 to 10 minutes. Remove from the heat and cool to room temperature; discard the bay leaf.

2. Position a rack in the middle of the oven and preheat the oven to 350 degrees F. In a large bowl, combine the ground veal and pork with the onion mixture, eggs, bread crumbs, salt and pepper and mix thoroughly. Set aside ¾ cup of the meat mixture. On a piece of waxed paper, pat the remaining meat mixture out into a rectangle about 8 inches by 20 inches and about 1 inch thick. Arrange the cheese slices over the ground meat layer, overlapping them if necessary to fit the rectangle exactly. Arrange the ham slices over the cheese, overlapping them slightly if necessary to fit. Beginning with a short side of the rectangle, and using the waxed paper as an aid, roll the rectangle into a round loaf. Seal the ends of the loaf by spreading the reserved meat mixture evenly over them. With the aid of the waxed paper, carefully transfer the loaf to a 9-by-5-by-3-inch loaf pan, positioning it with the seam side down.

3. Bake the loaf for about 1 hour and 20 minutes, pouring off accumulated pan juices from time to time. The meat loaf is done when an instant-reading thermometer inserted into the center registers 160 degrees F. Let rest for 10 minutes before slicing. Serve hot.

Creamed Mushrooms

Serves 6 to 8

This luscious skillet full of creamy mushrooms is as much sauce for the veal roulade loaf as it is a side dish. Various exotic, formerly wild, mushrooms are now cultivated and are increasingly found in supermarkets. Using more than one type of mushroom makes for a more complex flavor, but this is good even if you have nothing but ordinary white mushrooms.

3 pounds mixed fresh mushrooms such as shiitake, cremini and cultivated white
7 tablespoons unsalted butter
⅓ cup finely chopped shallots
1½ teaspoons salt
1 cup chicken stock or canned broth
¾ cup crème fraîche, whipping cream or heavy cream
2 tablespoons minced fresh thyme or 1 teaspoon dried
1 tablespoon unbleached all-purpose flour
1 tablespoon fresh lemon juice
1 teaspoon freshly ground black pepper

1. Trim the mushrooms, discarding the shiitake stems or reserving them for another use (such as stock). Wipe the mushrooms with a dampened paper towel. Halve or quarter the larger mushrooms; leave the smaller mushrooms whole.

2. In a large skillet, melt 6 tablespoons of the butter over low heat. Add the shallots and cook, stirring once or twice, until softened, 3 to 5 minutes. Stir in the mushrooms and raise the heat slightly. Cook covered, stirring once or twice, for 5 minutes. Uncover the skillet, stir in the salt and cook the mushrooms, stirring occasionally, for 5 minutes, or until the mushrooms have softened and rendered some of their juices.

3. Stir in the chicken stock, crème fraîche and thyme. Raise the heat, bringing the mushrooms to a brisk simmer and cook uncovered, stirring often, for about 7 minutes, or until the liquid has reduced slightly and the mushrooms are tender. In a small bowl, mash together the remaining 1 tablespoon butter and the flour. Whisk this paste into the mushrooms. Stir in the lemon juice and pepper and simmer for another 1 or 2 minutes, or until the sauce is thick. Serve hot.

■ ■ ■

Finishing touches: Accompany the meat loaf and creamed mushrooms with Classic Scalloped Spuds (page 127) or parslied white rice. Drink a well-balanced Chardonnay and provide plenty of crusty bread for mopping up the mushroom juices. Dessert should be something country club classy—chocolate mousse, for example, or vanilla ice cream topped with orange liqueur.

Cranberry-Glazed Turkey Loaf with a Tunnel of Stuffing

Serves 8

Unless you're a real meat loaf fanatic, it's unlikely that you'll actually serve this variation for Thanksgiving. Still, paired with the sweet potato side dish below, it covers all the tastes of America's favorite holiday meal, and when you want to recall that abundance without actually cooking up a turkey and all the trimmings, it's speedy and satisfying.

½ stick (4 tablespoons) unsalted butter
2 cups finely chopped onions
½ cup finely chopped celery
1 teaspoon poultry seasoning
1 bay leaf
2½ pounds ground turkey
3 eggs, beaten
½ cup rolled oats
1½ teaspoons salt
1 teaspoon freshly ground black pepper
1 box (6 ounces) top-of-the-stove stuffing, any flavor, prepared according to the package directions, or 3 cups homemade stuffing
1 container (12 ounces) Ocean Spray cranberry-orange Cran-Fruit Crushed Fruit

1. In a large skillet, melt the butter over medium heat. When it foams, add the onions, celery, poultry seasoning and bay leaf, cover and cook, stirring once or twice, until the vegetables are lightly colored, 8 to 10 minutes. Remove from the heat, discard the bay leaf and cool to room temperature.

2. Position a rack in the middle of the oven and preheat the oven to 350 degrees F. In a large bowl, combine the ground turkey, the onion mixture, eggs, oats, salt and pepper and mix thoroughly. Pat about half of the turkey mixture into the bottom of a long 9-cup loaf pan, such as a Pullman bread pan. With the back of a spoon, press a shallow trench in the turkey mixture, running the length of the pan. Fill the trench with the stuffing, using it all. Mound the remaining turkey mixture over the stuffing, enclosing the stuffing completely. Spread the crushed fruit evenly over the top of the loaf, using it all.

3. Bake for about 1¼ hours, or until an instant-reading thermometer inserted in the turkey portion of the loaf registers 160 degrees F. Let the loaf rest on a rack for 10 minutes before slicing. Serve hot.

Praline Sweet Potato Gratin

Serves 8

Baking the sweet potatoes carmelizes their natural sugars, adding extra flavor to the gratin, but you can boil the potatoes if you prefer. The potatoes can be cooked one day ahead. Topped with a crunchy pecan and brown sugar praline, the gratin reheats while the turkey loaf finishes baking.

4 pounds sweet potatoes (5 or 6 large)
1 stick (8 tablespoons) unsalted butter
1½ cups coarsely chopped pecans (about 6 ounces)
½ cup packed light brown sugar

1. Position a rack in the middle of the oven and preheat the oven to 400 degrees F. Pierce each potato several times with a fork. Lay the potatoes on the oven rack and bake until just tender, about 1 hour. When the potatoes are cool enough to handle comfortably, peel them. *The recipe can be prepared to this point 1 day ahead. Cool the potatoes completely, wrap well and refrigerate.*

2. Position a rack in the middle of the oven and preheat the oven to 350 degrees F. Butter a shallow 6-cup baking dish. Cut the potatoes into 1-inch chunks and arrange them evenly in the prepared dish.

3. In a medium saucepan, melt the butter over medium heat. Add the pecans and cook, stirring once or twice, for 3 minutes. Remove from the heat and stir in the brown sugar. Spoon the pecan mixture evenly over the sweet potatoes.

4. Bake for about 45 minutes, or until the potatoes are very tender and the praline topping is crisp and lightly browned. Serve hot.

■ ■ ■

Finishing touches: Serve the meat loaf with buttered brussels sprouts or Well-Cheddared Broccoli (page 79) and accompany it with corn muffins. The wine most often recommended with these contrasty, Thanksgiving flavors is a red zinfandel, but if you like white wines spicy Gewürztraminer works equally well. Serve pumpkin pie (what else?) for dessert.

Leftovers: This meat loaf is perfect for recreating the classic Thanksgiving leftover sandwich of turkey, stuffing and cranberry sauce. Lay one or two thin slices of the loaf on a piece of white bread, top with additional cranberry sauce (or mayonnaise or Miracle Whip, if preferred), add a second slice of white bread and enjoy.

Tarragon Chicken and Wild Mushroom Loaf with Dijon Potato Crust

Serves 8 to 10

Frosted with a thick layer of mustardy mashed potatoes, this loaf has the impressive appearance of baked Alaska, although in my opinion it is far tastier to eat. Since the meat and potatoes are combined in one dish, the actual last minute fussing in the kitchen is reduced and serving is simplified.

MEAT LOAF
5 tablespoons unsalted butter
2 cups finely chopped onions
1 tablespoon dried tarragon, crumbled
¾ pound shiitake mushrooms, stems discarded, coarsely chopped (about 4 cups)
2 teaspoons salt
2½ pounds ground chicken
3 eggs, beaten
½ cup rolled oats
1½ teaspoons freshly ground black pepper

POTATO CRUST
2½ pounds russet baking potatoes (4 to 5 large), peeled and chunked
3 teaspoons salt
⅔ cup milk
¼ cup Dijon-style mustard
3 tablespoons unsalted butter, softened
2 egg yolks, beaten
½ teaspoon freshly ground black pepper
½ cup finely chopped flat-leaf parsley

1. In a large skillet, melt the butter over medium heat. When it foams, add the onions and tarragon, cover and cook, stirring once or twice, until the onions are lightly colored, 8 to 10 minutes. Add the mushrooms and 1 teaspoon of the salt and cook uncovered, stirring once or twice, for 10 minutes. Remove from the heat and cool to room temperature.

2. Position a rack in the middle of the oven and preheat the oven to 350 degrees F. In a large bowl, combine the ground chicken with the mushroom mixture, eggs, oats, pepper and the remaining 1 teaspoon salt and mix thoroughly. Transfer to a shallow baking dish and form into a flat loaf; smoothing the top of the loaf with the back of a spoon.

3. Bake the loaf for 35 minutes. Meanwhile, in a large pan cover the potatoes with water. Stir in 2 teaspoons of the salt, set over medium heat and bring to a boil. Cook uncovered, stirring once or twice, until the potatoes are very tender, about 25 minutes. Drain the potatoes and force them through the medium disk of a food

Creamed Cauliflower with Ham

Serves 8 to 10

The pale white and green of the chicken and potato loaf is complemented by the pale white and pink of this side dish, and the combined flavors of chicken, tarragon, mushrooms, cauliflower, ham and mustard go wonderfully well together. Frozen cauliflower, cooked according to the package directions, can be substituted for the fresh vegetable.

1 large cauliflower (about 2½ pounds), separated into florets (about 8 cups)
2½ teaspoons salt
½ stick (4 tablespoons) unsalted butter
¼ pound firm, smoky baked ham, cut into ¼-inch dice (about ¾ cup)
3 tablespoons unbleached all-purpose flour
2 cups milk
½ teaspoon freshly ground black pepper

1. Bring a large pot of water to a boil. Stir in the cauliflower and 2 teaspoons of the salt and cook, stirring once or twice, until just tender, about 5 minutes. Drain immediately, transfer to a bowl of cold water and let stand until cool. Drain well. *The cauliflower can be cooked up to 1 day ahead. Wrap well and refrigerate.*

mill or mash them by hand; do not use a food processor. In a large bowl, combine the potatoes with the milk, mustard, butter and egg yolks. Stir in the remaining 1 teaspoon salt, the pepper and parsley and beat until fluffy.

4. Spread the warm potato mixture evenly over the hot chicken loaf. Return the loaf to the oven and bake for another 15 to 20 minutes, or until the potato crust is firm but not browned. An instant-reading thermometer inserted into the center of the loaf should register 145 degrees F. Let the loaf rest for 10 minutes on a rack before slicing. Serve hot.

2. In a large skillet, melt the butter over low heat. When it foams, add the ham and cook, stirring once or twice, until lightly colored, about 4 minutes. Whisk the flour into the skillet and cook, stirring once or twice, for 3 minutes. Slowly whisk in the milk. Raise the heat slightly and stir in the remaining ½ teaspoon salt, the pepper and the cauliflower. Cook partially covered, stirring often and basting the cauliflower with the sauce, until the sauce thickens slightly and the cauliflower is heated through, about 5 minutes. Adjust the seasoning and serve hot.

Finishing touches: Serve the chicken loaf and creamed cauliflower with good bread and follow with a green salad. Drink a crisp dry white wine, such as Sauvignon blanc. For dessert, the flavor combinations in this menu make me think, somehow, of apples—baked, for instance, and basted while cooking with maple syrup and orange marmalade.

Leftovers: The mashed potatoes make this loaf unsuitable as a sandwich filling, but, wrapped in foil and gently oven-warmed, it is delicious the next day as is.

Picadillo Loaf in a Cornmeal Crust

Serves 6 to 8

This hotly spiced, Cuban-influenced beef-and-pork loaf is studded with raisins, corn and green olives and baked under a steamy, golden cloak of corn bread. Admittedly, like other loaves in this chapter, this has more than a little of the artsy-craftsy about it, but despite—(or perhaps because of)—the manual dexterity called for, it's intriguing and delicious.

¼ cup olive oil
2 cups finely chopped onions
4 garlic cloves, minced
½ teaspoon dried oregano, crumbled
¼ teaspoon crushed hot red pepper
1 pound ground beef
1 pound hot, Italian-style sausage, removed from the casing and crumbled
¾ cup canned or defrosted corn kernels, well drained
½ cup fine, dry, seasoned bread crumbs
2 eggs, beaten
½ cup sliced pimiento-stuffed green olives
⅓ cup raisins
1 teaspoon salt
Cornmeal Crust (recipe follows)

1. In a large skillet, warm the olive oil over medium heat. Add the onions, garlic, oregano and hot pepper. Cover and cook, stirring once or twice, until tender, 8 to 10 minutes. Remove from the heat and cool to room temperature.

2. Position a rack in the middle of the oven and preheat the oven to 350 degrees F. In a large bowl, combine the ground beef, sausage, onion mixture, corn, bread crumbs, eggs, olives, raisins and salt and blend well. Transfer the meat mixture to a shallow baking dish and shape it into an oval loaf about 2½ inches high; smooth the top with the back of a spoon.

3. Bake for 1 hour. Drain off any juices from the baking dish. Spread the cornmeal batter evenly over the hot picadillo loaf. Return the loaf to the oven and bake for 25 minutes longer, or until the cornmeal crust is set and an instant-reading thermometer inserted into the center of the meat loaf registers 160 degrees F. Let the loaf rest on a rack for 10 minutes before slicing. Serve hot.

Cornmeal Crust

This batter can also be used to make a good, basic corn bread. Spoon it into a buttered 8- or 9-inch square pan and bake it at 400 degrees F for 25 minutes, or until a tester inserted into the center comes out clean.

1 cup yellow cornmeal
1 cup unbleached all-purpose flour
2½ tablespoons sugar
2 teaspoons baking powder
1 teaspoon freshly ground black pepper
¼ teaspoon salt
1 cup buttermilk, at room temperature
½ stick (4 tablespoons) unsalted butter, melted
1 egg

1. In a large bowl, stir together the cornmeal, flour, sugar, baking powder, pepper and salt.

2. In a small bowl, whisk together the buttermilk, melted butter and egg. Add the buttermilk mixture to the cornmeal mixture and stir until just combined. Use immediately.

Cumin Black Beans

Serves 6 to 8

Other beans, such as pinto or red kidney, can be substituted in this easy, colorful side dish. For more fire, sauté a minced fresh jalapeño along with the red bell pepper.

1 pound dried black (turtle) beans, picked over to
    remove any grit
2¾ teaspoons salt
¼ cup olive oil
1 large red bell pepper, finely chopped
2 garlic cloves, minced
2 teaspoons ground cumin
1 teaspoon dried oregano, crumbled
5 green onions, sliced
1 cup chicken stock or canned broth
½ teaspoon freshly ground black pepper

1. In a large bowl, combine the beans with enough cold water to cover them by at least 3 inches and let stand overnight. Drain the beans. In a large pot, combine the beans with enough cold water to cover them by at least 3 inches and set over medium heat. When the water boils, lower the heat and simmer the beans, partially covered, for 20 minutes. Stir in 2 teaspoons of the salt and cook for another 15 to 20 minutes, or until the beans are just tender. Drain immediately. *The beans can be prepared to this point 1 day ahead. Cool to room temperature, cover and refrigerate.*

2. In a large skillet, warm the olive oil over medium heat. Add the bell pepper, garlic, cumin and oregano, cover and cook, stirring once or twice, for 6 minutes. Add the green onions, cover and cook for 4 minutes. Add the beans, chicken stock, the remaining ¾ teaspoon salt and the black pepper. Raise the heat slightly and cook uncovered, tossing and stirring the beans, until they are heated through and have absorbed most of the chicken broth, 3 to 4 minutes. Serve hot.

■ ■ ■

Finishing touches: Serve the picadillo loaf and the black beans with the Tomato, Avocado and Lettuce Salad on page 29. Drink a cold beer. For dessert, serve a caramel custard.

Leftovers: The best way to enjoy leftovers of this meat loaf is to wrap slices in plastic and reheat them in a microwave oven.

Chapter Six

ALTERNATIVE LOAF STYLES

Recipes for the Times in Which We Live

The times, they are a changing. Never before have so many thought for so long and hard about nearly everything they eat. Sugar is out, fiber is in, cholesterol is everywhere, but then cholesterol is not half so bad as fat, which is in even more places (including our middles) than cholesterol. Oat bran was good, then it wasn't and now it's good again, but wheat and rice bran are good, too. Is rice bran something you can buy? Who knows!?

Broccoli is in, grains are in, beans are really in. While many people have realized that eating all three may be embarrassing at times, they fear that skipping all three could have dire conse-quences on their arteries and other cherished internal systems. Turkey is very in, and so is chicken and seafood, not to mention their increasing political correctness. Who wants dinner to be divine if it includes as its major ingredient A Dwindling World Resource?

Is there a place for meat loaf in all this nutritional turmoil? But of course, as the following modern meat loaf alternatives—some low on fat and cholesterol, others low on endangered species, all of them long on the hearty flavor and moist, satisfying texture—prove.

Salmon Loaf with Basil Sauce

Serves 6 to 8

This new-age loaf is not a rich, smooth and sophisticated seafood mousse. Rather it is as coarsely textured, moist and satisfying to eat as any good red meat leaf would be. The sauce can also be made with fresh dill or tarragon.

¾ stick (6 tablespoons) unsalted butter
2 cups finely chopped onions
2 pounds boneless, skinless fresh salmon, well chilled
¾ cup saltine cracker crumbs
2 eggs, beaten
1 tablespoon Dijon-style mustard
1 tablespoon Worcestershire sauce
2½ teaspoons salt
1½ teaspoons freshly ground black pepper
3 tablespoons unbleached all-purpose flour
1 cup fish stock or bottled clam juice
½ cup dry white wine
¼ cup whipping cream or heavy cream
3 tablespoons finely chopped fresh basil

1. In a large skillet, melt 4 tablespoons of the butter over medium heat. When it foams, add the onions, cover and cook, stirring once or twice, until tender and lightly colored, 8 to 10 minutes. Remove from the heat and cool to room temperature.

2. Position a rack in the middle of the oven and preheat the oven to 350 degrees F. Lightly butter a 9-by-5-by-3-inch loaf pan. Cut the salmon into 1-inch chunks. In a food processor, with short bursts of power, chop the salmon. Do not puree; some texture, like that of coarsely ground meat, should remain.

3. In a large bowl, combine the salmon, the cooked onions, cracker crumbs, eggs, mustard, Worcestershire sauce, 2 teaspoons of the salt and 1 teaspoon of the pepper and blend well. Transfer the salmon mixture to the prepared pan, mounding it slightly; smooth the top of the loaf with the back of a spoon. Set the loaf pan into a larger pan (like a roaster) and add enough very hot tap water to the large pan to reach halfway up the sides of the loaf pan.

4. Set this hot water bath into the oven and bake for 50 minutes, or until an instant-reading thermometer inserted into the center of the loaf registers 120 degrees F. Let the salmon loaf rest in the water bath, on a rack, while preparing the sauce.

5. In a medium saucepan, melt the remaining 2 tablespoons butter over low heat. Whisk in the flour and cook, stirring often, for 3 minutes. Whisk in the fish stock, wine, and remaining ½ teaspoon each salt and pepper and bring to a boil. Lower the heat slightly and cook uncovered, stirring and skimming the sauce, for 4 minutes, or until thickened. Stir in the cream and basil and cook for another minute.

6. Slice the salmon loaf and serve it hot, napped with the sauce.

1. In a small skillet, melt the butter over low heat. When it foams, add the green onions, cover and cook, stirring once or twice, for about 4 minutes, or until very tender. Remove from the heat and stir in the parsley.

2. Meanwhile, bring a pot of lightly salted water to a boil. Add the lima beans and cook uncovered, stirring once or twice, until very tender, about 5 minutes; drain.

3. In a food processor, combine the lima beans, green onion mixture and chicken broth and puree until smooth. Add the salt and pepper and process again to blend. *The puree can be prepared several hours head, and held, loosely covered, at room temperature. Warm over low heat, stirring often, until steaming, about 4 minutes. Serve hot.*

■ ■ ■

Parslied Lima Bean Puree

Serves 6 to 8

Lima beans have great flavor, but some people dislike the texture. This puree is the solution to that food phobia, and the creamy, pale green and entirely unctuous results of a few minutes spent in the food processor might well have lima beans replacing mashed potatoes as the meat loaf side dish of choice.

3 tablespoons unsalted butter
⅔ cup sliced green onions
⅓ cup finely chopped flat-leaf parsley
3 packages (10 ounces each) frozen Fordhook lima
    beans, thawed
⅓ cup chicken stock or canned broth
1½ teaspoons salt
1 teaspoon freshly ground black pepper

Finishing touches: Serve the salmon loaf and lima puree with Cherry Tomato Sauté (page 101) or buttered baby carrots. Corn bread goes well with this menu, and a low alcohol, not too dry Chardonnay would be a good wine choice. Serve a strawberry tart or other fresh fruit-based pastry for dessert.

Leftovers: The salmon loaf makes a great cold sandwich, spread with mayonnaise into which a bit of prepared pesto sauce has been stirred.

Hearty Chicken Loaf with Whole Wheat Crumbs

Serves 6 to 8

In this full-flavored alternative loaf, the toasted whole wheat crumbs are more than mere filler; their quantity and nutty taste make them an important flavor and texture element as well. The crumbs also give the loaf an unusual "tweedy" appearance. It is a nice change from the usual kind, its hearty flavor doing much to convert red meat eaters to the possibilities of poultry.

1¼ cups fresh crumbs from a 100-percent whole grain, health food store–type bread (do not use soft supermarket sandwich loaves)
¼ cup olive oil
2 large leeks (white part only), well cleaned and finely chopped (about 2 cups)
1 medium red bell pepper, finely chopped (about 1 cup)
2 garlic cloves, minced
2 pounds ground chicken
2 eggs, beaten
½ cup chicken stock or canned broth
2 teaspoons salt
1 teaspoon freshly ground black pepper

1. Position a rack in the middle of the oven and preheat the oven to 400 degrees F. Spread the bread crumbs in a shallow metal pan (like a cake tin) and toast them in the oven, stirring often, until lightly browned, about 10 minutes. Cool to room temperature. Lower the oven temperature to 350 degrees F.

2. In a large skillet, warm the olive oil over medium heat. Add the leeks, bell pepper and garlic. Cover and cook, stirring occasionally, until the vegetables are tender and lightly colored, 8 to 10 minutes. Remove from the heat and cool to room temperature.

3. In a large bowl, combine the ground chicken, the leek mixture, the toasted crumbs, eggs, chicken stock, salt and pepper and blend well. Transfer the meat mixture to a 9-by-5-by-3-inch loaf pan, mounding it slightly; smooth the top with the back of a spoon.

4. Bake the loaf for about 50 minutes, or until an instant-reading thermometer inserted into the center or the loaf registers 160 degrees F. Let the loaf rest on a rack for 10 minutes before slicing. Serve hot.

Shiitake Mushroom Rice

Serves 6 to 8

This loosely creamy rice is reminiscent of the great Italian dish, risotto, minus the essential imported ingredient (Arborio rice) and the pressure on the cook (almost constant stirring). Prepared with the increasingly available exotic mushrooms known as shiitake, it's a delicious, complexly flavored affair.
Made with ordinary cultivated white mushrooms (use ¾ pound and do not discard the stems), it's less unusual, but no less rich and satisfying.

¾ stick (6 tablespoons) unsalted butter
1 cup finely chopped onion
2 garlic cloves, minced
1 teaspoon dried marjoram, crumbled
3 cups chicken stock or canned broth
2 teaspoons salt
1 cup long-grain white rice
1 pound shiitake mushrooms, stems discarded, caps
    coarsely chopped
½ teaspoon freshly ground black pepper
⅓ cup minced flat-leaf parsley

1. In a medium saucepan, melt 3 tablespoons of the butter over medium heat. When it foams, add the onion, garlic and marjoram. Cover and cook, stirring once or twice, until tender and lightly colored, 8 to 10 minutes. Add 2½ cups of the stock and 1 teaspoon of the salt and bring to a boil. Stir in the rice, turn the heat to low, cover and cook without disturbing for 20 minutes. There will be some liquid not absorbed by the rice.

2. Meanwhile, in a large skillet, melt the remaining 3 tablespoons butter over medium heat. Add the mushrooms, cover and cook, stirring once or twice, for 4 minutes. Season with the remaining 1 teaspoon salt and cook, covered, stirring once or twice, for 4 minutes longer, or until the mushrooms begin to render their juices. Add the remaining ½ cup stock to the skillet, raise the heat slightly and simmer uncovered, stirring once or twice, for about 5 minutes, or until the liquid in the skillet is reduced by about half and the mushrooms are tender.

3. Add the rice with its liquid to the mushrooms in the skillet. Bring to a simmer and cook, stirring often, until the rice has absorbed most—but not all—of the mushroom liquid, 2 to 3 minutes. The mixture should remain somewhat saucy. Stir in the pepper and parsley, remove from the heat, cover and let stand for 1 minute. Serve hot.

■ ■ ■

Finishing touches: Accompany the chicken loaf and the mushroom rice with Gingered Baby Carrots (page 51) or Cherry Tomato Sauté (page 101). Any crusty good bread would be appropriate and a California Chardonnay would be a fine wine choice. For dessert, serve lemon sorbet or sherbet, with a pureed blueberry or raspberry sauce.

Leftovers: Make a sandwich of thin slices of this meat loaf, plus lettuce and juicy tomatoes, on more of that same hearty whole grain bread used in the meat loaf.

Shrimp and Chicken Loaf with Pink Tomato Cream

Serves 6 to 8

Chicken and shrimp (or, sometimes, crayfish) are an honorable combination, showing up together in various cuisines. They seem to enhance each other, with tasty results, as this loaf with its creamy pink sauce will illustrate. The theme may be meat loaf, but the finished product, thanks to the inclusion of shrimp and a sophisticated sauce, is rather festive. Serve this at a dinner party, not as a quick supper at the end of a long and busy day.

¾ stick (6 tablespoons) unsalted butter
1½ cups finely chopped onions
½ cup finely chopped celery
2 garlic cloves, minced
1 pound medium shrimp, shelled, deveined and well chilled
1 pound ground chicken
½ cup fine, dry, seasoned bread crumbs
2 eggs, beaten
2 ounces Jarlsberg or Swiss cheese, grated (about ½ cup)
2½ teaspoons salt

1 teaspoon freshly ground black pepper
1 can (14 ounces) plum tomatoes, crushed and drained
1 cup chicken stock or canned broth
½ cup whipping cream or heavy cream
¼ teaspoon sugar
2 tablespoons unbleached all-purpose flour

1. In a large skillet, melt 4 tablespoons of the butter over medium heat. When it foams, add the onions, celery and garlic. Cover and cook, stirring once or twice, until the vegetables are tender and lightly colored, 8 to 10 minutes. Remove from the heat and cool to room temperature.

2. Position a rack in the middle of the oven and preheat the oven to 350 degrees. Lightly butter a 9-by-5-by-3-inch loaf pan. In a food processor, with short bursts of power, chop the shrimp. Do not puree; some texture, like that of coarsely ground meat, should remain. In a large bowl, combine the shrimp, ground chicken, the onion mixture, bread crumbs, eggs, cheese, 2 teaspoons of the salt and the pepper and blend well. Transfer the shrimp mixture to the prepared pan, mounding it slightly; smooth the top of the loaf with the back of a spoon. Set the loaf pan into a larger pan (like a roaster) and add enough very hot tap water to the large pan to reach half-way up the sides of the loaf pan.

4. Set this hot water bath into the oven and bake for 1 hour, or until an instant-reading thermometer inserted into the center of the loaf registers 130 degrees F. Let the shrimp loaf rest in the water bath, on a rack, while preparing the sauce.

5. In a medium nonreactive saucepan, combine the tomatoes, chicken stock, cream, the remaining ½ teaspoon salt and the sugar. Bring to a simmer over low heat. Cook uncovered, stirring occasionally, for about 12 minutes, or until reduced by about one-fourth. In a small bowl, mash together the remaining 2 tablespoons butter and the flour. Bit by bit, whisk this paste into the sauce. Simmer for about 2 minutes, stirring often, until the sauce is thick.

6. Slice the shrimp loaf and serve it hot, napped with the sauce.

Lemon-Parsley New Potatoes

Serves 6 to 8

Seek out the smallest possible potatoes (about 1 inch in diameter) for this recipe. Then they are not only delicious, they are also eye-appealing, and look particularly good puddled by the shrimp loaf's creamy pink sauce.

2½ pounds small red-skinned new potatoes (about 24), scrubbed.
¾ stick (6 tablespoons) unsalted butter
⅓ cup finely chopped flat-leaf parsley
1 tablespoon minced lemon zest (colored peel)
½ teaspoon salt
½ teaspoon freshly ground black pepper

1. With a swivel-bladed vegetable peeler, remove a ¼-inch-wide strip from around the middle of each potato. In a large saucepan, cover them with cold, lightly salted water and set over medium heat. Bring to a boil and cook about 9 minutes, or until just tender; drain. *The potatoes can be prepared to this point several hours ahead. Cover and hold at room temperature.*

2. In a large skillet, melt the butter over low heat. Add the potatoes, cover and cook, rolling the potatoes in the hot butter, until they are heated through and lightly browned, about 6 minutes. Sprinkle the parsley, lemon zest, salt and pepper over the potatoes and remove from the heat. Transfer the potatoes to a serving dish, pour the butter from the pan over them and serve hot.

■ ■ ■

Finishing touches: Serve the shrimp and chicken loaf and the new potatoes with lightly buttered fresh asparagus. Accompany them with tiny hot biscuits and drink a California Chardonnay. Dessert might be fresh fruit, like melon and blueberries, sauced with a little orange juice and honey.

Leftovers: This is a firm loaf and leftovers can be cut into ¾-inch cubes and scattered over a vinaigrette-dressed green salad.

Lean Turkey Loaf with Caramelized Vegetables

Serves 6 to 8

Browning the aromatic vegetables in the oven requires only a spritz from a can of no-stick spray, but the process creates a lot of deep rich flavor in this spa-style loaf. Egg whites contribute little cholesterol, lean turkey white meat is low in fat (especially if you chop your own), and the resulting loaf, while qualifying as diet food, is hearty and satisfying. (If you are avoiding sodium, use a low-salt chicken broth and unsalted bread crumbs and reduce the added salt or omit it altogether.)

Pam, or other no-stick cooking spray
1 medium onion, quartered
2 large carrots, peeled and chunked
4 large whole shallots, peeled
⅓ cup chicken stock or canned broth
2 pounds boneless turkey breast, skin removed, meat cut into 1-inch chunks and well chilled
¾ cup fine, dry, seasoned bread crumbs
3 egg whites, whisked until foamy
2 teaspoons salt
1 teaspoon freshly ground black pepper
½ teaspoon dried thyme leaves, crumbled

1. Position a rack in the middle of the oven and preheat the oven to 400 degrees F. Lightly spray a shallow glass baking dish (such as a pie plate) with Pam. Arrange the onion, carrots and shallots in the plate; coat the vegetables lightly with the cooking spray. Bake the vegetables, turning them once or twice, until lightly browned all over, about 45 minutes. Cool slightly. Reduce the oven temperature to 350 degrees F. In a food processor, combine the browned vegetables and chicken stock and puree until almost smooth.

2. Lightly spray a 9-by-5-by-3-inch loaf pan with Pam. In the food processor (no need to clean it), with short bursts of power, chop the turkey. Do not puree it; some texture, like that of coarsely ground meat, should remain. In a large bowl, combine the chopped turkey, vegetable puree, bread crumbs, egg whites, salt, pepper and thyme and blend well. Transfer the mixture to the prepared pan, mounding it slightly; smooth the top with the back of a spoon.

3. Bake the loaf for about 50 minutes, or until an instant-reading thermometer inserted into the center of the loaf registers 160 degrees F. Let the loaf rest on a rack for 10 minutes before slicing. Serve hot.

Orange-Flavored Brown Rice with Asparagus

Serves 6 to 8

This recipe combines both vegetable and starch in a single tasty, colorful, low-fat dish. Though this will be better if you use "Jubilee" or one of the other increasingly available gourmet rice blends grown and packaged by the Lundberg family of Richvale, California, plain—but not converted—brown rice can be substituted. For low-sodium diets, just reduce or omit the salt.

1½ pounds asparagus, trimmed and cut on an angle into 1-inch pieces
4 cups water
2½ teaspoons salt
2 cups brown rice, rinsed
⅓ cup fresh orange juice, strained
2 tablespoons finely minced orange zest (colored peel)
1 teaspoon freshly ground black pepper

1. Bring a large saucepan of lightly salted water to a boil over high heat. Add the asparagus and cook, stirring once or twice, until the asparagus turns bright green and is crisp/tender, about 4 minutes (the water need not even return to the boil). Drain and transfer immediately to a large bowl of very cold water. Cool completely and drain well. *The asparagus can be prepared several hours in advance. Wrap well and hold at room temperature.*

2. In a medium saucepan, bring the water to a boil over medium heat. Stir in the salt and then the brown rice. Cover the pan, reduce the heat to low and cook undisturbed until the rice is tender and has absorbed all the water, about 45 minutes.

3. Stir the asparagus, orange juice, orange zest and pepper into the brown rice and let stand, covered, for 3 minutes. Fluff with a fork and serve hot.

■ ■ ■

Finishing touches: Accompany the turkey loaf and brown rice with a hearty multi-grain bread (toasted, if desired, for extra texture and flavor). Drink fresh fruit juice with a splash of soda water. For dessert, serve a sauce of pureed mangos, sweetened with honey, over a compote of pitted sweet black cherries.

Leftovers: Cut leftover turkey loaf into small cubes; mix with chunks of apple and celery, dress with yogurt and sprinkle with chopped walnuts to make a kind of turkey Waldorf salad.

Reduced Fat, Lower Cholesterol Beef Loaf

Serves 6 to 8

Fish, chicken and turkey loaves are all very well, but sometimes only beef will do. While it will never quite qualify as health food, the following red meat loaf, using a few fat- and cholesterol-lowering tricks, at least makes a nod toward modern nutritional concerns. It is satisfyingly moist and flavorful, too.

1 cup coarsely grated zucchini
2 teaspoons salt
1½ cups finely chopped onions
½ cup Egg Beaters or other egg substitute
½ cup plus ⅓ cup ketchup
1½ tablespoons Worcestershire sauce
1 tablespoon hot pepper sauce
1 tablespoon Dijon-style mustard
3 garlic cloves, crushed through a press
½ teaspoon freshly ground black pepper
½ teaspoon dried thyme leaves, crumbled
½ teaspoon dried oregano, crumbled
2 pounds very lean ground beef
½ cup fine, dry, seasoned bread crumbs

1. In a strainer set over a bowl, combine the grated zucchini and 1 teaspoon of the salt and let stand, stirring once or twice, for 30 minutes. With your hands squeeze as much liquid out of the zucchini as possible.

2. In a large bowl, stir together the onions, zucchini, Egg Beaters, ½ cup of the ketchup, the Worcestershire sauce, hot pepper sauce, mustard, garlic, remaining 1 teaspoon salt, black pepper, thyme and oregano. Add the beef and bread crumbs and mix thoroughly to blend well. Transfer the meat mixture to a 9-by-5-by-3-inch loaf pan (use a double meat loaf pan with a perforated liner if you wish, to drain away any fatty juices) and pack it firmly into a loaf. Smooth the top of the loaf with the back of a spoon. Spread the remaining ⅓ cup ketchup evenly over the loaf.

3. Bake the meat loaf for about 1 hour, or until an instant-reading thermometer inserted into the center barely registers 145 degrees F. Let the meat loaf rest on a rack for 10 minutes before slicing.

Sally Schneider's Amazing Buttermilk Mashed Potatoes

Serves 6 to 8

This recipe, adapted from Sally's award-winning book *The Art of Low-Calorie Cooking* (Stewart, Tabori & Chang), really is amazing. Leaving the skins on adds extra flavor and texture, the low-fat buttermilk and the baking soda interact to lighten the potatoes and the small amount of butter added at the end creates that all-important, luxurious "mouth feel" mashed potato-lovers crave. For an additional buttery boost (one more psychological than actual), use one of the increasingly available yellow-fleshed potato varieties, such as Yukon Gold or Finnish.

2½ pounds all-purpose white potatoes, unpeeled and
    well scrubbed (or peeled, if desired)
1½ cups warmed buttermilk
1 teaspoon baking soda
1 tablespoon plus 1 teaspoon unsalted butter,
    softened
1 teaspoon salt
1 teaspoon freshly ground black pepper

1. In a large saucepan, cover the potatoes with lightly salted cold water and set over medium-high heat. Bring to a boil and cook, stirring once or twice, until tender, about 45 minutes. Drain, reserving about ⅓ cup of the cooking water.

2. Transfer the potatoes to a large bowl and mash with a potato masher or fork until fairly smooth, leaving as many lumps as desired. Combine the buttermilk and baking soda and beat the mixture into the potatoes with a wooden spoon until thoroughly incorporated. For creamier potatoes, gradually beat in the reserved cooking water until the desired texture is reached. Stir in the butter, salt and pepper. Serve hot.

■ ■ ■

Finishing touches: Accompany the leaner loaf and the amazing potatoes with steamed broccoli or another green vegetable of your choice. Serve hearty whole grain bread and drink a light beer (only one!). For dessert, enjoy seasonal fresh fruit. After dinner, take a walk.

Leftovers: The meat loaf makes a nice sandwich the next day. Try it on toasted whole grain bread, spread with a bit of low-fat or low-cholesterol mayonnaise, or your favorite mustard.

Chapter Seven

FAST FOOD

Recipes from the Back of the Box

We're in a hurry, we're hungry and we're ready for a little home cooking. Unfortunately, after Black Monday we cut up our credit cards and let the housekeeper go, which means that nowadays when we speak of home cooking, we're talking about actually cooking! At home! *My broker told me there would be days like this. Is there a solution to eating well (eating comfortably) when the wolf's at the door and the rat race is at your heels? The good news is yes. The better news is that the recipes for some of the world's best, easiest, cheapest and quickest meat loaves are printed on the backs of boxes, cans, cartons and bags. Meat loaves are rarely hard work, but such convenience recipes are designed to save you even more time in the kitchen by substituting the product in question (canned soup, corn flakes, mayonnaise) for some time-consuming kitchen task or other. Combined with the economical nature of meat loaves in general, these back-of-the-box formulas result in remarkably quick, wonderfully homemade-tasting meat loaves, every bit as good as the ones Mom made—probably right off the back of the box.*

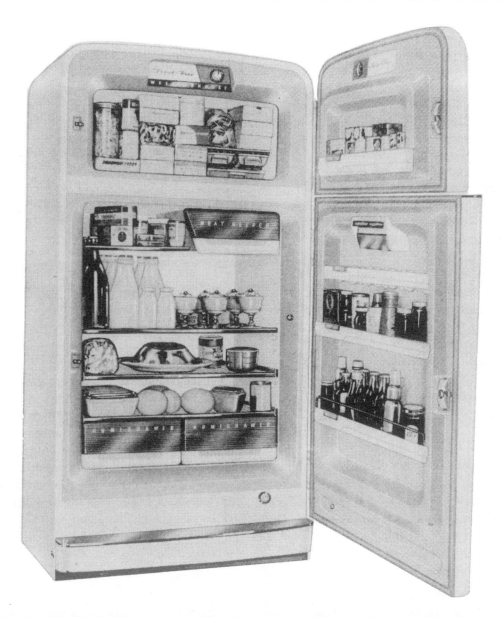

Lipton Souperior Meat Loaf

Serves 6 to 8

The intensely concentrated onion powder packed into an envelope of Lipton soup mix fairly explodes into savory flavor when baked into the following meat loaf. One of several classic back-of-the-box recipes from the soup mix folks, it's had a profound effect on the meat loaf industry; many a savvy meat loaf maker now knows to reach for the Lipton soup mix when the pressure is on. There are more complicated meat loaves, but few that are tastier.

2 pounds ground beef
1½ cups soft, fresh bread crumbs
2 eggs, beaten
1 envelope Lipton Onion, Beefy Onion or Beefy Mush-
    room Recipe Soup Mix
¾ cup water
⅓ cup ketchup
1 teaspoon freshly ground black pepper

1. Position a rack in the middle of the oven and preheat the oven to 350 degrees F.

2. In a large bowl, combine the ground beef, bread crumbs, eggs, soup mix, water, ketchup and pepper and blend well. Transfer the mixture to a shallow baking pan and form it into a loaf about 2½ inches thick.

3. Bake the loaf for about 1 hour, or until an instant-reading thermometer inserted into the center of the loaf registers 145 degrees F. Let the loaf rest on a rack for 10 minutes before slicing. Serve hot.

Classic Scalloped Spuds

Serves 6 to 8

Except for my addition of a generous measure of buttery sautéed onions, these potatoes are pretty much the ones my mother made about as often as she made mashed—which is to say more or less daily. The recipe doesn't need to be richer, but you can replace some or all of the milk with whipping cream or heavy cream if you wish.

¾ stick (6 tablespoons) unsalted butter
2 medium onions, very thinly sliced
4½ pounds russet baking potatoes (8 to 9 large),
   thinly sliced
2 teaspoons salt
1 teaspoon freshly ground black pepper
1¾ cups milk

1. In a large skillet, melt 4 tablespoons of the butter over medium heat. When it foams, add the onions, cover and cook, stirring once or twice, until tender and lightly colored, 8 to 10 minutes. Remove from the heat.

2. Put the potatoes in a large pot and cover with lightly salted cold water. Set the pan over medium heat and bring to a boil, stirring occasionally. Cook the potatoes for 1 minute, then drain them into a colander and rinse well under cold running water.

3. Position a rack in the middle of the oven and preheat the oven to 350 degrees F. Lightly butter a deep 3-quart casserole. Arrange one-third of the potatoes in the prepared casserole. Spread half of the sautéed onions over the potatoes. Season with one-third of the salt and one-third of the pepper. Spread half the remaining potatoes over the onion layer. Spread the remaining onions over the potato layer and season with half of the remaining salt and pepper. Spread the remaining potatoes over the onion layer. Season with the remaining salt and pepper and dot with the remaining 2 tablespoons butter. Pour the milk evenly over the potatoes.

4. Bake the casserole for about 1½ hours, occasionally tipping and tilting the dish to baste all the potatoes with the milk, or until the potatoes are tender, the top is lightly browned and the potatoes have absorbed most of the milk. Let the casserole rest on a rack for 10 minutes before serving. Serve hot.

■ ■ ■

Finishing touches: Serve the meat loaf and the creamy potatoes with a plain green vegetable, such as steamed broccoli. Accompany the meal with freshly baked yeast rolls. For dessert, offer homemade cookies and fresh fruit.

Leftovers: This meat loaf has such an immediately recognizable, homemade taste, its leftovers are best enjoyed, like most classic meat loaves, in a white bread sandwich moistened with a little ketchup.

Emergency Pantry Meat Loaf

Serves 6 to 8

Even back-of-the-package meat loaves take an hour or so to bake (although dividing the mixture between small loaf pans or muffin cups can shave 30 minutes off that time), so the issue here is not so much speed as spontaneity. Blessed by a pantry stocked with meat loaf essentials, the only really fresh item you'll need the next time company calls on the car phone to tell you they're arriving just in time for dinner is the ground beef—which I hope you'll have enough sense to ask them to pick up for you at the next market they pass. (If they also bring you a package of bacon, halve 4 slices crosswise and arrange them, overlapping slightly, atop the ketchup, just before the loaf goes into the oven.)

1 bag (12 ounces) frozen chopped onions, thawed, with their juices
1 jar (7 ounces) roasted red peppers, drained and finely chopped
½ cup mayonnaise
1 tablespoon Worcestershire sauce
2 teaspoons chopped garlic (from a jar is fine)
1 teaspoon hot pepper sauce
1 teaspoon salt
2 pounds ground beef

¾ cup fine, dry bread crumbs
⅓ cup ketchup, barbecue sauce or chili sauce

1. Position a rack in the middle of the oven and preheat the oven to 350 degrees F. In a large bowl, whisk together the onions, roasted peppers, mayonnaise, Worcestershire sauce, garlic, hot pepper sauce and salt. Crumble the ground beef into the bowl. Add the bread crumbs and mix thoroughly. Transfer the meat mixture to a 9-by-5-by-3-inch loaf pan, mounding it slightly; smooth the top with the back of a spoon. Spread the ketchup evenly over the meat loaf.

2. Bake the meat loaf for about 1 hour and 20 minutes, pouring off the accumulated pan juices occasionally, until an instant-reading thermometer inserted into the center registers 145 degrees F. Let the loaf rest on a rack for 10 minutes before slicing. Serve hot.

Elegant Freezer Vegetable Sauté

Serves 6 to 8

The vegetable section of a typical supermarket freezer case is full of surprises these days. When did carrots, peas and corn get joined by such stylish and offbeat company as asparagus, artichoke hearts, snow peas, pureed squash, collard greens and black-eyed peas? While not every one of these vegetables survives freezing with equal success, teaming them lets the strengths of one compensate for the weaknesses of another. And when sauced with good butter and fresh lemon, and seasoned liberally with the spice of convenience, the following mélange of formerly frozen greenery makes a more than adequate partner to the best meat loaf you can manage.

¾ stick (6 tablespoons) unsalted butter
1 cup frozen chopped onion
1 package (10 ounces) frozen asparagus, thawed and
    drained
1 package (10 ounces) frozen baby lima beans, thawed
    and drained
1 package (10 ounces) frozen peas with baby onions,
    thawed and drained
1 package (9 ounces) frozen artichoke hearts, thawed
    and drained
½ cup chicken stock or canned broth
1 teaspoon salt
¾ teaspoon freshly ground black pepper
2 tablespoons fresh lemon juice
¼ cup finely chopped flat-leaf parsley (optional)

1. In a large sauté pan or flameproof casserole, melt the butter over low heat. When it foams, add the onion, cover and cook, stirring once or twice, for 10 minutes.

2. Add the asparagus, lima beans, peas and onions, artichoke hearts, chicken stock, salt and pepper. Cover and cook, stirring gently once or twice, for about 5 minutes, or until the vegetables are heated through and have absorbed some of the stock. Stir in the lemon juice and sprinkle the vegetables with the parsley, if you are using it. Serve hot.

■ ■ ■

Finishing touches: Serve the spontaneous meat loaf and vegetable sauté with simple baked potatoes, topped with butter and sour cream. Drink an uncomplicated red wine, such as Beaujolais, or stick to beer and soft drinks if the occasion is an informal one. In this impromptu menu, dessert purchased from a good bakery makes perfect sense.

Leftovers: This meat loaf makes a wonderful sandwich, served on a Vienna- or Italian-type bread (crusty outside, soft within), spread liberally with both ketchup and mayonnaise.

Kellogg's Spicy Tomato Mini-Loaves

Serves 6

This back-of-the-box recipe from the Kellogg Kitchens inspires serious nostalgia in me, since it very much resembles the one my mother made for the family when I was growing up. I can still see her prudently setting aside her wedding ring on the window sill by the sink before mixing the corn flakes into the meat mixture by hand. These little free-form mini-loaves are easy to shape (the kids can help) and they bake up very quickly—perfect at the end of a busy day.

1½ pounds ground beef
3 cups Kellogg's Corn Flakes cereal
1 can (10¾ ounces) condensed tomato soup
¼ cup finely chopped onion
1 egg, beaten
1 tablespoon prepared white horseradish
2 tablespoons packed light brown sugar
1 teaspoon Dijon-style mustard

1. Position a rack in the middle of the oven and preheat the oven to 350 degrees F. In a large bowl, combine the ground beef, corn flakes, half of the condensed soup, onion, egg and horseradish and mix thoroughly. Divide the meat mixture into 6 equal portions. On a foil-lined jelly roll sheet pan, shape each portion into a round or oval loaf. Mix together the remaining soup, brown sugar and mustard. Spead evenly over the loaves.

2. Bake for about 35 minutes, or until an instant-reading thermometer inserted into the center of a loaf registers 145 degrees F. Let the loaves rest on a rack for 5 minutes before serving.

Green Bean Casserole

Serves 6 to 8

I would be the last person to challenge the supremacy of the green bean casserole recipe from Campbell's—you know, the one with the condensed mushroom soup and the canned onion rings. After the hamburger and, possibly, the chocolate chip cookie, that venerable back-of-the-box classic is probably cooked up more often than any other single dish in America. Still, when you're looking for a change of pace (one with only a little extra work involved), try this tart, creamy variation, adapted from the Kellogg Kitchens. You may slice and sauté fresh mushrooms, if you wish, and stir them into the sauce along with the green beans.

¾ stick (6 tablespoons) unsalted butter
½ cup finely chopped onion
¼ cup unbleached all-purpose flour
2 teaspoons sugar (optional)
2 teaspoons salt
1 teaspoon freshly ground black pepper
2 cartons (8 ounces each) reduced-fat sour cream
8 cups French-cut frozen green beans, thawed and
    well drained
1 cup Kellogg's Corn Flake Crumbs

1. Position a rack in the upper third of the oven and preheat the oven to 350 degrees F. Butter a shallow, 3-quart baking dish. In a large saucepan, melt 4 tablespoons of the butter over low heat. Stir in the onion, flour, sugar, salt and pepper. Whisk in the sour cream. Cook, stirring occasionally, until thick, about 3 minutes. Stir in the green beans. Transfer the mixture to the prepared baking dish. *The recipe can be prepared to this point several hours ahead. Cover and hold at room temperature.*

2. Sprinkle the corn flake crumbs over the bean mixture. Melt the remaining 2 tablespoons butter and drizzle it over the corn flake crumbs. Bake for about 35 minutes, or until the filling is bubbling and the topping is lightly browned. Let the casserole rest on a rack for 5 minutes before serving.

■ ■ ■

Finishing touches: Serve this menu with any potato dish of your choice—perhaps something prepared on the top of the stove, since the oven(s) will be busy. For dessert, offer something hearty and homemade—pie, cookies or cake—or offer a choice of fresh fruit.

Leftovers: Sticking with the nostalgia theme, I would enjoy these meat loaves sliced thin, on white sandwich breast, anointed with a splash of ketchup.

Vegetable Confetti Meat Loaf

Serves 6 to 8

Onion soup is not the only convenient Lipton flavor-booster available to meat loaf makers. Here is a loaf I devised using that company's vegetable recipe soup mix. Chock full of various veggies, it adds a completely different taste and texture to easy, old-fashioned back-of-the-box meat loaf.

1 cup sour cream
1 envelope Lipton Vegetable Recipe Soup Mix
¼ cup water
1 pound ground beef
½ pound ground pork
½ pound ground veal
¾ cup fine, dry bread crumbs
2 eggs, beaten
1 teaspoon freshly ground black pepper
⅓ cup ketchup
4 slices of bacon, halved crosswise

1. In a small bowl, whisk together the sour cream, soup mix and water. Let stand at room temperature, stirring once or twice, for 30 minutes.

2. Position a rack in the middle of the oven and preheat the oven to 350 degrees F. In a large bowl, combine the ground beef, pork and veal with the sour cream mixture, bread crumbs, eggs and pepper; blend well. Transfer the mixture to a 9-by-5-by-3-inch loaf pan, mounding it slightly. Spread the ketchup atop the loaf. Arrange the bacon strips, overlapping them slightly, atop the ketchup.

3. Bake the meat loaf for about 1 hour and 20 minutes, or until an instant-reading thermometer inserted into the center registers 160 degrees F. Let the loaf rest on a rack for 10 minutes before slicing.

Potatoes and Corn au Gratin

Serves 6 to 8

Two favorite starches, corn and potatoes, pair up again in this rich and creamy side dish. Other cheeses, such as cheddar or jalapeño Monterey Jack, can replace the Swiss.

3 pounds russet baking potatoes (4 or 5 large), peeled and thinly sliced
¾ teaspoon salt
1 package (10 ounces) frozen corn kernels, thawed and drained
5 ounces soft herb and garlic-flavored cheese, such as Boursin
6 ounces Swiss cheese, grated (about 1½ cups)
¾ teaspoon freshly ground black pepper
1¼ cups chicken stock or canned broth
¾ cup whipping cream or heavy cream

1. Position a rack in the middle of the oven and preheat the oven to 350 degrees F. Butter a deep 3-quart casserole.

2. Arrange one-third of the potatoes in the bottom of the prepared casserole. Season with ¼ teaspoon of the salt. Scatter half of the corn over the potato layer. Dot the corn layer with half of the herb cheese. Scatter one-third of the grated Swiss cheese over the corn. Season with ¼ teaspoon of the pepper. Arrange half of the remaining potatoes in the casserole. Season with another ¼ tea-

spoon salt. Scatter the remaining corn over the potatoes. Dot the corn with the remaining herb cheese. Scatter half of the remaining Swiss cheese over the corn. Season with ¼ teaspoon pepper. Arrange the remaining potatoes in the casserole. Pour the chicken stock and cream evenly over the casserole. Season the top potato layer with the remaining ¼ teaspoon each salt and pepper. Scatter the remaining Swiss cheese over the potatoes.

3. Bake the casserole for about 1½ hours, or until the potatoes have absorbed most of the liquid, the top is browned and the cheeses are melted and bubbling. Let the casserole rest for 10 minutes on a rack before serving.

■ ■ ■

Finishing touches: Serve the meat loaf and au gratin potatoes with a colorful vegetable, such as buttered peas and carrots or broiled tomatoes. For dessert, bake—or buy—a lemon meringue pie.

Leftovers: Try this loaf sliced thin, sandwiched with cheddar cheese on whole grain bread, and cooked on a griddle until the cheese melts. Serve it with warmed chili sauce, barbecue sauce or ketchup.

Campbell's Meat Loaf Wellington

Serves 6 to 8

Not all back-of-the-box recipes are simple. This one, a retro relic of the Fifties, when such elegant, complicated fare as Beef Wellington was in vogue, is an example of how busy things in the kitchen can get. Wrapped in a crust of refrigerator crescent roll dough, this meat loaf only echoes the genuine article (which calls for puff pastry, duxelles of mushrooms and pâté de foie gras), but it's still a hoot to assemble. If dough-wrapped meat loaves are too much for you, just remember that under that crust is Campbell's delicious Best Ever Meat Loaf, a back-of-the-box classic. So maybe you should just serve the crescent rolls on the side?

1 can (10¾ ounces) Campbell's Condensed Cream of
    Mushroom or Golden Mushroom Soup
2 pounds ground beef
½ cup fine, dry bread crumbs
1 egg, beaten
⅓ cup finely chopped onion
1 teaspoon salt
1 package (8 ounces) refrigerator crescent dinner
    rolls, separated
⅓ cup water

1. Position a rack in the middle of the oven and preheat the oven to 375 degrees F. In a large bowl, thoroughly mix together ½ cup of the soup, the ground beef, bread crumbs, egg, onion and salt. Transfer the meat mixture to a shallow baking dish and shape firmly into an 8-by-4-inch loaf about 3 inches high.

2. Bake for 1 hour. Pour off the drippings, reserving 3 tablespoons. Place the dinner roll dough crosswise over the top and down the sides of the meat loaf, overlapping the pieces slightly. Bake the loaf for another 15 minutes, or until the dough is puffed and golden. Let the meat loaf rest on a rack for 10 minutes before slicing.

3. Meanwhile, in a saucepan, combine the remaining soup, the ⅓ cup water and the reserved meat drippings. Heat, stirring occasionally, until simmering. Serve the gravy with the meat loaf.

Twice-Baked Potatoes

Serves 8

If you're going to make a complicated meat loaf you might as well make a slightly complicated side dish. These potatoes aren't really difficult, just *manipulated*. The baked spuds are hollowed out, re-stuffed with a puree of mashed potato and green peas, then baked up hot and steamy under a goo of cheese, a state of affairs that somehow makes all that manipulation worthwhile.

8 large russet baking potatoes (10 to 12 ounces each), well scrubbed
Vegetable or olive oil
2 packages (10 ounces each) frozen peas, thawed and drained
¼ cup whipping cream or heavy cream
½ stick (4 tablespoons) unsalted butter, softened
2 teaspoons salt
1 teaspoon freshly ground black pepper
4 ounces Jarlsberg cheese, grated (about 1 cup)

1. Position a rack in the middle of the oven and preheat the oven to 400 degrees F. Prick each potato several times with a fork. Rub the skins with oil, set the potatoes directly on the oven rack and bake until very tender, about 1 hour.

2. Cool the potatoes on a rack until they are comfortable to handle. Cut off the top of each potato and spoon out the flesh, leaving a shell with sides about ¼ inch thick.

Force the warm potato flesh and the peas through the medium disk of a food mill set over a medium bowl or through a ricer. Beat the cream, butter, salt and pepper into the potato mixture. *The recipe can be prepared to this point 1 day ahead. Cover and refrigerate the filling and the potato shells separately, returning them to room temperature before proceeding.*

3. Position a rack in the middle of the oven and preheat the oven to 375 degrees F. Spoon the mashed potato mixture evenly into the potato shells, mounding it and using it all. Set the filled potatoes in a shallow baking dish and bake for about 30 minutes, or until hot. Sprinkle the grated cheese over the filling and return the potatoes to the oven until the cheese melts and bubbles, about 5 minutes. Let the potatoes rest on a rack for 5 minutes before serving.

■ ■ ■

Finishing touches: Serve the meat loaf *en croûte* and the stuffed potatoes with Cherry Tomato Sauté (page 101). Drink a good (but not a great) California Cabernet Sauvignon, and serve chocolate mousse for dessert.

Leftovers: The crust makes this meat loaf a poor candidate for leftover status, unless you want to remove and discard it—then use the meat loaf inside for sandwiches, salads and so on.

Heinz Red Magic Meat Loaf

Serves 6

It would hardly be honest for a meat loaf cookbook to omit a meat loaf from Heinz, the ketchup makers to America. This is a tasty little loaf, one I have adapted slightly to include ground pork, which harmonizes particularly well with the pineapple atop the loaf. If you're dealing with big eaters, or want leftovers, double this.

1 pound ground beef
½ pound ground pork
1 cup soft, fresh bread crumbs
⅓ cup plus ¼ cup Heinz Tomato Ketchup
¼ cup finely chopped onion
1 egg, beaten
½ teaspoon salt
½ teaspoon freshly ground black pepper
¼ cup drained crushed canned pineapple

1. Position a rack in the middle of the oven and preheat the oven to 350 degrees F. In a large bowl, mix together the ground beef and pork with the bread crumbs, ⅓ cup of the ketchup, the onion, egg, salt and pepper. Transfer the meat mixture to an 8-by-4-by-2½-inch pan, mounding it slightly; smooth the top with the back of a spoon.

2. Bake the loaf for 50 minutes. In a small bowl, mix together the remaining ¼ cup ketchup and the pineapple. Spread the pineapple mixture over the loaf and bake for another 30 minutes, or until an instant-reading thermometer inserted into the center registers 160 degrees F. Let the loaf rest on a rack for 10 minutes before slicing.

Lipton's Creamy Baked Mashed Potatoes

Serves 6 to 8

These mashed potatoes, adapted from the Lipton Kitchens, pick up flavor and a spangling of vegetables from the packet of instant soup stirred into them, and since they get assembled ahead and bake in the oven along with the meat loaf, your last minute kitchen fussing is reduced and simplified.

2½ pounds russet baking potatoes (about 4 large), peeled and chunked
1¼ cups milk
1 cup grated Swiss or mild cheddar cheese
1 envelope Lipton Vegetable Recipe Soup Mix
½ cup sliced green onions
1 egg, beaten

1. Position a rack in the middle of the oven and preheat the oven to 350 degrees F. Lightly butter a 1½-quart baking dish.

2. In a large saucepan, cover the potatoes with cold, lightly salted water. Set over medium heat and bring to a boil. Cook uncovered, stirring once or twice, until very tender, about 20 minutes. Drain the potatoes.

3. Mash the potatoes by hand or in a ricer or force them through the medium disk of a food mill; do not use a food processor. In a large bowl, beat together the mashed potatoes and milk. Stir in ¾ cup of the cheese, the soup mix, green onions and egg. Spoon the mixture into the prepared baking dish.

4. Bake the potatoes for 50 minutes, or until they are firm and the top is lightly colored. Sprinkle the remaining ¼ cup cheese over the potatoes and bake for another 5 minutes, or until the cheese melts. Let the casserole stand on a rack for 5 minutes before serving.

■ ■ ■

Finishing touches: Serve the meat loaf and baked mashed potatoes with a simple green vegetable like buttered broccoli or green beans. This easy, middle-of-the-week menu deserves a simple dessert, like purchased sherbet or fresh fruit and bakery cookies.

Leftovers: The meat loaf reheats nicely in foil, in the oven, and is delicious as is or on a sandwich of crusty plain or onion bread.

Quick and Easy
Ranch Loaf

Serves 6 to 8

Always on the lookout for the ideal, instant flavor-booster that makes meat loaf magic, I turned one day to a packet of ranch-type dressing mix. Full of buttermilk, garlic and herb flavors, it proved to be a speedy and easy way to achieve my goal: a hot, moist and savory loaf with the minimum of work. If your supermarket does not offer ready-ground meat loaf blend (50 percent beef, 25 percent pork, 25 percent veal), you can substitute all beef, though the load will lack slightly in both the flavor and texture departments.

½ cup milk
1 package (1 ounce) Hidden Valley Original Ranch
    Salad Dressing Mix
1 pound ground beef
½ pound ground pork
½ pound ground veal
½ cup fine, dry, seasoned bread crumbs
2 eggs, beaten
1 teaspoon freshly ground black pepper
⅓ cup ketchup
4 slices of bacon, halved crosswise

1. Position a rack in the middle of the oven and preheat the oven to 350 degrees F. In a small bowl, stir together the milk and dressing mix and let stand for 5 minutes. In a large bowl, combine the ground beef, pork and veal with the milk mixture, bread crumbs, eggs and pepper and blend well. Transfer the meat mixture to a 9-by-5-by-3-inch loaf pan, mounding it slightly; smooth the top of the loaf with the back of a spoon. Spread the ketchup evenly over the loaf. Arrange the bacon pieces, overlapping them slightly if necessary, atop the ketchup.

3. Bake the meat loaf for about 1 hour, or until an instant-reading thermometer inserted into the center of the loaf registers 145 degrees F. Let the loaf rest on a rack for 10 minutes before slicing. Serve hot.

Watercress Salad

Serves 6 to 8

At Mortimer's, an Upper East Side Manhattan society hangout, the meat loaf recipe, which was borrowed from designer Bill Blass, remains a house secret, but the accompaniment, a crisp, green watercress salad, seems like such a good idea I have borrowed it for my ranch dressing loaf (I admit the association of salad dressing and salad greens also was inspirational). Whether the meat loaf is hot, warm or cold, the tart, peppery salad is a fine and crunchy partner.

4 bunches of watercress, trimmed, rinsed and patted dry
½ cup plus 2 tablespoons olive oil
½ teaspoon salt
2½ tablespoons red wine vinegar
½ teaspoon freshly ground black pepper

1. In a large bowl, toss the watercress with the olive oil. Add the salt and toss again. Add the vinegar and pepper and toss thoroughly. Adjust the seasoning, adding more salt, vinegar or pepper to taste. Serve immediately.

Finishing touches: Good bread is all this meat loaf and salad really requires by way of accompaniment, although if you would like to further duplicate the Mortimer's experience, spoon a dollop of hot pepper jelly onto the plate next to the loaf. Drink a good beer or a glass of cool, uncomplicated red wine; a Spanish rioja would be an excellent choice. For dessert, try butterscotch pudding.

Leftovers: Dice the cold meat loaf and toss it with salad greens, coarsely chunked tomatoes, sliced hard-cooked eggs and crisp bacon bits. Add a dressing of your choice, ranch dressing being particularly appropriate.

INDEX

A

Acorn squash, baked maple-rum, 35
Ann Landers's good advice meat loaf, 78
Apple(s)
  -pear sauce, 37
  pork loaf with cheese and, 34
  scrapple, 18
Artichoke hearts, in elegant freezer vegetable sauté, 129
Asparagus
  with brown rice, orange-flavored, 121
  in elegant freezer vegetable sauté, 129
Avocado, tomato, and lettuce salad, 29

B

Bacon, beef and blue cheese mini-muffin loaves with, 100
Barley, in baked four-grain dressing with mushrooms, 65
Basil
  in pesto mashed potatoes, 47
  rice salad with peas and pine nuts, 43
  sauce, salmon loaf with, 114
BBQ chicken loaf, firecracker, 20
Bean(s)
  baked, hot and smoky, 87
  black
    and beef loaf, salsa-topped, 28
    cumin, 111
  white, and cucumber and tomato salad with feta and fresh mint, 49
Beef
  all-beef loaves
    Ann Landers's good advice meat loaf, 78
    beef and blue cheese mini-muffin loaves with bacon, 100

beef, sausage and spinach loaf with tomato-olive sauce, 45
chutney-glazed curried beef loaf, 54
classic interstate meat loaf, 16
the dream loaf, 74
Ed Debevic's burnt diner meat loaf, 88
emergency pantry meat loaf, 128
Kellogg's spicy tomato mini-loaves, 130
Lipton souperior meat loaf, 126
Little Italy pepperoni-mushroom pizza loaf, 32
New England corned beef loaf, 26
reduced fat, lower cholesterol beef loaf, 122
salsa-topped beef and black bean loaf, 28
Serendipity 3's country meat loaf, 90
Campbell's meat loaf Wellington, 134
mixed-meat loaves
  egg-in-the-middle meat loaf, 98
  the El Paso Chile Company's Tex-Mex meat loaf, 80
  Germantown meat loaf with sauerkraut, horseradish and dill, 36
  Good Enough To Eat's Upper West Side meat loaf, 84
  Heinz red magic meat loaf, 136
  Leonard Schwartz's Maple Drive and 72 Market Street meat loaf, 92
  Paul Prudhomme's Cajun meat loaf, 82
  picadillo loaf in a cornmeal crust, 109
  pretty much pâté, 40
  quick and easy ranch loaf, 138
  Rick Rodgers's ballpark meat loaf, 86
  smoked three-meat loaf, 62

  two-meat meat loaf with sun-dried tomatoes, 60
  vegetable confetti meat loaf, 132
Beets, Harvard, 27
Black bean(s)
  and beef loaf, salsa-topped, 28
  cumin, 111
Blue cheese and beef mini-muffin loaves with bacon, 100
Brandied cherry sauce, venison ring with, 64
Broccoli, well-cheddared, 79
Brown rice
  with asparagus, orange-flavored, 121
  in baked four-grain dressing with mushrooms, 65
Bulgur and lamb loaf with yogurt sauce, Eastern Mediterranean, 48
Buttermilk
  mashed potatoes, Sally Schneider's amazing, 123
  meat loaf, herb garden, 70

C

Cabbage
  red, sweet and sour, 63
  white
    coleslaw, charcuterie, 41
    sauerkraut, Germantown meat loaf with horseradish, dill and, 36
Cajun meat loaf, Paul Prudhomme's, 82
Campbell's meat loaf Wellington, 134
Cannellini. *See* White bean(s)
Caramelized vegetables, lean turkey loaf with, 120
Carrot(s)
  baby, gingered, 51
  caramelized, lean turkey loaf with, 120

and glazed ham mosaic loaf, 72
and peas, creamed, 99
and rutabaga and shallot pudding, 53
Cauliflower with ham, creamed, 107
Celery root and potato gratin, 59
Charcuterie coleslaw, 41
Cheddar cheese
  pork loaf with apples and, 34
  well-cheddared broccoli, 79
Cheese
  au gratin, potatoes and corn, 133
  blue cheese and beef mini-muffin loaves
      with bacon, 100
  cheddar
    pork loaf with apples and, 34
    well-cheddared broccoli, 79
  chèvre, veal and roasted red pepper
      loaf with baked garlic gravy, 67
  easy macaroni and, for a crowd, 85
  feta, in white bean, cucumber and to-
      mato salad with fresh mint, 49
  grits, with hot sausage and onions,
      baked, 83
Cherry sauce, brandied, venison ring with,
    64
Cherry tomato sauté, 101
Chèvre, veal and roasted red pepper loaf
    with baked garlic gravy, 67
Chicken (loaf)
  firecracker BBQ, 20
  in herb garden buttermilk meat loaf, 70
  pressed, Hazel's, 24
  and shrimp loaf with pink tomato
      cream, 118
  tarragon and wild mushroom, with
      Dijon potato crust, 106
  with whole wheat crumbs, hearty, 116
Church supper salad, 25
Chutney-glazed curried beef loaf, 54
Classic interstate meat loaf, 16
Classic scalloped spuds, 127
Coleslaw, charcuterie, 41
Cordon bleu roulade, veal, 102
Corn(meal)
  creamed fresh, 17
  crust, 110
  picadillo loaf in a crust of, 109
  polenta, peppery pan-grilled, 61

potatoes and, au gratin, 133
-rosemary batter, zucchini and eggplant
    fritters in, 94
Corned beef loaf, New England, 26
Cracked wheat. See Bulgur
Cranberry-glazed turkey loaf with a tunnel
    of stuffing, 104
Cream(-ed,-y)
  cauliflower with ham, 107
  dilled pan gravy, Swedish meat loaf
      with, 52
  mushrooms, 103
  peas and carrots, 99
  shrimp and chicken loaf with pink to-
      mato, 118
Cucumber, white bean and tomato salad
    with feta and fresh mint, 49
Cumin black beans, 111
Curried beef loaf, chutney-glazed, 54

D
Dijon potato crust, tarragon chicken and
    wild mushroom loaf with, 106
Dill(ed)
  creamy pan gravy, Swedish meat loaf
      with, 52
  Germantown meat loaf with sauerkraut,
      horseradish and, 36
Double mushroom pork and veal loaf with
    fresh thyme, 58
Dream loaf, the, 74

E
Eastern Mediterranean lamb and bulgur
    loaf with yogurt sauce, 48
Ed Debevic's burnt diner meat loaf, 88
Ed's caramelized onion stuff, 89
Egg(s)
  -in-the-middle meat loaf, 98
  and potato salad with sweet pickles,
      state fair, 21
  scrambled with toast, 19
Eggplant and zucchini fritters in rose-
    mary-cornmeal batter, 94
El Paso Chile Company's Tex-Mex meat
    loaf, the, 80
Emergency pantry meat loaf, 128

F
Fennel, braised, 69
Feta cheese, white bean, cucumber and
    tomato salad with fresh mint
    and, 49
Firecracker BBQ chicken loaf, 20
Fish. See Salmon; Tuna
Four-grain dressing with mushrooms,
    baked, 65
Fritters, zucchini and eggplant, in rose-
    mary-cornmeal batter, 94
Fruit
  apple(s)
    -pear sauce, 37
    pork loaf with cheese and, 34
    scrapple, 18
  cranberry-glazed turkey loaf with a tun-
      nel of stuffing, 104
  orange-flavored brown rice with aspara-
      gus, 121
  pineapple luau loaf, 30

G
Garlic gravy, veal roasted red pepper and
    chèvre loaf with baked, 67
Germantown meat loaf with sauerkraut,
    horseradish and dill, 36
Gingered baby carrots, 51
Goat cheese. See Chèvre
Good Enough To Eat's Upper West Side
    meat loaf, 84
Gratin
  potato and celery root, 59
  potatoes and corn au, 133
  praline sweet potato, 105
Gravy
  baked garlic, veal, roasted red pepper
      and chèvre loaf with, 67
  creamy dilled pan, Swedish meat loaf
      with, 52
Green bean(s)
  casserole, 131
  lemon, 71
Grits with hot sausage and onions, baked
    cheese, 83

H

Ham
   creamed cauliflower with, 107
   and carrot mosaic loaf, glazed, 72
   and pork loaf with sweet mustard glaze,
     Millie's, 22
Harvard beets, 27
Hazel's pressed chicken loaf, 24
Heinz red magic meat loaf, 136
Herb garden buttermilk meat loaf, 70
Horseradish, Germantown meat loaf with
   sauerkraut, dill and, 36

K

Kellogg's spicy tomato mini-loaves, 130

L

Lamb and bulgur loaf with yogurt sauce,
   Eastern Mediterranean, 48
Landers's, Ann, good advice meat loaf, 78
Lemon
   green beans, 71
   -parsley new potatoes, 119
Lentils with peas and tomatoes, spicy, 55
Leonard Schwartz's Maple Drive and 72
   Market Street meat loaf, 92
Lettuce, tomato and avocado salad, 29
Lima bean(s)
   baby, in elegant freezer vegetable
     sauté, 129
   puree, parslied, 115
Lipton's creamy baked mashed potatoes,
   137
Lipton souperior meat loaf, 126

M

Macadamia sugar snap peas, 31
Maple-rum baked squash, 35
Mayonnaise, tuna, 43
   cold veal loaf with, 42
Millie's pork and ham loaf with sweet
   mustard glaze, 22
Mint, fresh, white bean, cucumber and tomato salad with feta and, 49
Mushroom(s)
   baked four-grain dressing with, 65
   creamed, 103
   -pepperoni pizza loaf, Little Italy, 32

pork and veal loaf with fresh thyme,
   double, 58
shiitake rice, 117
wild, and tarragon chicken loaf with
   Dijon potato crust, 106
Mustard
   Dijon potato crust, tarragon chicken
     and wild mushroom loaf with,
     106
   glaze, Millie's pork and ham loaf with
     sweet, 22

N

New England corned beef loaf, 26

O

Olive-tomato sauce, 46
   beef, sausage and spinach loaf with, 45
Onion(s)
   baked cheese grits with hot sausage
     and, 83
   stuff, Ed's caramelized, 89
Orange-flavored brown rice with asparagus, 121

P

Pan gravy, Swedish meat loaf with creamy
   dilled, 52
Parsley(-ied)
   -lemon new potatoes, 119
   lima bean puree, 115
Pasta
   bow ties with zucchini and roasted red
     peppers, 33
   macaroni and cheese for a crowd, easy,
     85
Paul Prudhomme's Cajun meat loaf, 82
Pear-apple sauce, 37
Peas
   with baby onions, in elegant freezer
     vegetable sauté, 129
   basil rice salad with pine nuts and, 43
   and carrots, creamed, 99
   lentils with tomatoes and, spicy, 55
   sugar snap, macadamia, 31
Pepperoni-mushroom pizza loaf, Little
   Italy, 32
Peppers(s), roasted sweet bell red

and veal and chèvre loaf with baked
   garlic gravy, 67
   pasta bow ties with zucchini and, 33
Peppery pan-grilled polenta, 61
Pesto mashed potatoes, 47
Picadillo loaf in a cornmeal crust, 109
Pickles, state fair potato and egg salad
   with sweet, 21
Pilaf, Rio Grande, 81
Pineapple luau loaf, 30
Pine nuts, basil rice salad with peas and,
   43
Pizza loaf, Little Italy pepperoni-mush-
   room, 32
Polenta, peppery pan-grilled, 61
Pork. *See also* Sausage
   all-pork loaves
     with apples and cheese, 34
     pineapple luau loaf, 30
   apple scrapple, 18
   mixed-meat loaves
     double mushroom pork and veal loaf
       with fresh thyme, 58
     the dream loaf, 74
     egg-in-the-middle meat loaf, 98
     the El Paso Chile Company's Tex-Mex
       meat loaf, 80
     Germantown meat loaf with sauer-
       kraut, horseradish and dill, 36
     Good Enough To Eat's Upper West
       Side meat loaf, 84
     Heinz red magic meat loaf, 136
     herb garden buttermilk meat loaf, 70
     Paul Prudhomme's Cajun meat loaf,
       82
     pork and ham loaf with sweet mus-
       tard glaze, Millie's, 22
     pretty much pâté, 40
     quick and easy ranch loaf, 138
     Rick Rodgers's ballpark meat loaf, 86
     smoked three-meat loaf, 62
     Swedish meat loaf with creamy dilled
       pan gravy, 52
     vegetable confetti meat loaf, 132
Potato(es)
   baked, twice-, 135
   and celery root gratin, 59
   classic scalloped spuds, 127

and corn au gratin, 133
Dijon crust, tarragon chicken and wild mushroom loaf with, 106
and egg salad with sweet pickles, state fair, 21
mashed, the, 75
  cakes, 23
  Lipton's creamy baked, 137
  pesto, 47
  Sally Schneider's amazing buttermilk, 123
new, lemon-parsley, 119
Praline sweet potato gratin, 105
Pretty much pâté, 40
Pudding, rutabaga, carrot and shallot, 53

Q
Quick and easy ranch loaf, 138
Quinoa, in baked four-grain dressing with mushrooms, 65

R
Red cabbage, sweet and sour, 63
Rice
  brown
    with asparagus, orange-flavored, 121
    in baked four-grain dressing with mushrooms, 65
  white
    pilaf, Rio Grande, 81
    salad with peas and pine nuts, basil, 43
    shiitake mushroom rice, 117
Rick Rodgers's ballpark meat loaf, 86
Rio Grande pilaf, 81
Rosemary-cornmeal batter, zucchini and eggplant fritters in, 94
Roulade, veal cordon bleu, 102
Rum-maple baked squash, 35
Rutabaga, carrot and shallot pudding, 53

S
Salad
  church supper, 25
  potato and egg with sweet pickles, state fair, 21
  rice with peas and pine nuts, basil, 43
  tomato, avocado and lettuce, 29

watercress, 139
white bean, cucumber and tomato, with feta and fresh mint, 49
Sally Schneider's amazing buttermilk mashed potatoes, 123
Salmon loaf with basil sauce, 114
Salsa-topped beef and black bean loaf, 28
Sauce. *See also* Gravy
  basil, salmon loaf with, 114
  brandied cherry, venison ring with, 64
  tomato-olive, 46
    beef, sausage and spinach loaf with, 45
  yogurt, Eastern Mediterranean lamb and bulgur loaf with, 48
Sauerkraut, Germantown meat loaf with horseradish, dill and, 36
Sausage
  andouille, baked cheese grits with onions and, 83
  Italian-style sweet
    beef, sausage and spinach loaf with tomato-olive sauce, 45
    in picadillo loaf in a cornmeal crust, 109
    in two-meat meat loaf with sun-dried tomatoes, 60
    in Leonard Schwartz's Maple Drive and 72 Market Street meat loaf, 92
    pepperoni-mushroom pizza loaf, Little Italy, 32
    scrapple, apple, 18
Schwartz's, Leonard, Maple Drive and 72 Market Street meat loaf, 92
Serendipity 3's country meat loaf, 90
Sherried teriyaki turkey loaf, 50
Shiitake mushroom rice, 117
Shrimp and chicken loaf with pink tomato cream, 118
Smoked three-meat loaf, 62
Spicy lentils with peas and tomatoes, 55
Spinach
  and beef and sausage loaf with tomato-olive sauce, 45
  sautéed, 73
Squash, baked maple-rum, 35

State fair potato and egg salad with sweet pickles, 21
Stuffing. *See also* Dressing
  cranberry-glazed turkey loaf with a tunnel of, 104
Sugar snap peas, macadamia, 31
Sun-dried tomatoes, two-meat meat loaf with, 60
Swedish meat loaf with creamy dilled pan gravy, 52
Sweet and sour red cabbage, 63
Sweet potato(es)
  fries, 91
  gratin, praline, 105

T
Tarragon chicken and wild mushroom loaf with Dijon potato crust, 106
Teriyaki turkey loaf, sherried, 50
Tex-Mex meat loaf, the El Paso Chile Company's, 80
Thyme, double mushroom pork and veal loaf with fresh, 58
Toast, eggs scrambled with, 19
Tomato(es)
  and avocado and lettuce salad, 29
  cherry, sauté, 101
  cream, shrimp and chicken loaf with, pink, 118
  lentils with peas and, spicy, 55
  -olive sauce, 46
    beef, sausage and spinach loaf with, 45
  and white bean and cucumber salad, with feta and fresh mint, 49
Tuna mayonnaise, 43
  cold veal loaf with, 42
Turkey (loaf)
  cranberry-glazed, with a tunnel of stuffing, 104
  lean, with caramelized vegetables, 120
  sherried teriyaki, 50
Two-meat meat loaf with sun-dried tomatoes, 60

V

Veal
  double mushroom pork loaf, with fresh
      thyme, 58
  the dream loaf, 74
  egg-in-the-middle meat loaf, 98
  Germantown meat loaf with sauerkraut,
      horseradish and dill, 36
  Good Enough To Eat's Upper West Side
      meat loaf, 84
  herb garden buttermilk meat loaf, 70
  Paul Prudhomme's Cajun meat loaf, 82
  pretty much pâté, 40
  quick and easy ranch loaf, 138
  and roasted red pepper and chèvre loaf
      with baked garlic gravy, 67
  roulade, cordon bleu, 102
  smoked three-meat loaf, 62
  Swedish meat loaf with creamy dilled
      pan gravy, 52
  with tuna mayonnaise, cold, 42
  vegetable confetti meat loaf, 132
Vegetable(s)
  artichoke hearts, in elegant freezer veg-
      etable sauté, 129
  asparagus
    with brown rice, orange-flavored, 121
    in elegant freezer vegetable sauté,
      129
  beets, Harvard, 27
  broccoli, well-cheddared, 79
  cabbage
    coleslaw, charcuterie, 41
    red, sweet and sour, 63
    sauerkraut, Germantown meat loaf
      with horseradish, dill and, 36
  caramelized, lean turkey loaf with, 120
  carrots

  baby, gingered, 51
  caramelized, lean turkey loaf with,
      120
  and glazed ham mosaic loaf, 72
  and peas, creamed, 99
  and rutabaga and shallot pudding, 53
cauliflower with ham, creamed, 107
confetti meat loaf, 132
corn
  creamed, fresh, 17
  and potatoes au gratin, 133
eggplant and zucchini fritters in rose-
    mary-cornmeal batter, 94
fennel, braised, 69
freezer, elegant sauté, 129
green bean(s)
  casserole, 131
  lemon, 71
mushroom(s)
  baked four-grain dressing with, 65
  creamed, 103
  -pepperoni pizza loaf, Little Italy, 32
  pork and veal loaf with fresh thyme,
      double, 58
  shiitake rice, 117
  wild, and tarragon chicken loaf with
      Dijon potato crust, 106
peas
  with baby onions, in elegant freezer
      vegetable sauté, 129
  basil rice salad with pine nuts and,
      43
  and carrots, creamed, 99
  lentils with tomatoes and, spicy, 55
  sugar snap, macadamia, 31
peppers(s), roasted sweet bell red
  and veal and chèvre loaf with baked
      garlic gravy, 67

  pasta bow ties with zucchini and, 33
potatoes. See Potato(es)
rutabaga, carrot and shallot pudding,
    53
spinach
  -beef and sausage loaf with tomato-
      olive sauce, 45
  sautéed, 73
zucchini
  and eggplant fritters, in rosemary-
      cornmeal batter, 94
  pasta bow ties with roasted red pep-
      pers and, 33
Venison ring with brandied cherry sauce,
    64

W

Watercress salad, 139
Well-cheddared broccoli, 79
Wheat berries, in baked four-grain dress-
    ing with mushrooms, 65
White bean, cucumber and tomato salad
    with feta and fresh mint, 49
Whole wheat crumbs, hearty chicken loaf
    with, 116
Wild mushroom and tarragon chicken loaf
    with Dijon potato crust, 106

Y

Yogurt sauce, Eastern Mediterranean
    lamb and bulgur loaf with, 48

Z

Zucchini
  and eggplant fritters in rosemary-corn-
      meal batter, 94
  pasta bow ties with roasted red peppers
      and, 33